THE COMPl

FARMING HANDBOOK

A Comprehensive Guide for Beginners and Experts On Shrimp Farming with A Step-By-Step Strategies for Designing Your Ponds, Feeding, Hatchery and Water Management

Jerrell J. Brady

All rights reserved. No part of this publication may be reproduced, distributed, or transmitted in any form or by any means, electronic, mechanical, photocopying, recording, or otherwise, without the prior written permission of the publisher, except in cases of brief quotations for use in critical reviews and other noncommercial uses permitted by copyright law.

Copyright ©Jerrell J. Brady, 2024.

CHAPTER 1
INTRODUCTION TO SHRIMP FARMING 8

1.1 History and Evolution of Shrimp Farming 8
- 1.1.1 Global Growth and Industrialization 9
- 1.1.2 The Role of Innovation...10
- 1.1.3 Sustainability Concerns and Reforms 11
- 1.1.4 The Future of Shrimp Farming..12

1.2 Overview of Shrimp Species for Farming 13
- 1.2.1 Whiteleg Shrimp (Litopenaeus vannamei) 14
- 1.2.2 Giant Tiger Prawn (Penaeus monodon) 15
- 1.2.3 Other Species..16
- 1.2.3 Species Selection Based on Location 17
- 1.2.4 Growth Rates and Yields 18
- 1.2.5 Choosing the Right Species for Beginners 19

1.3 Key Concepts in Aquaculture 20
- 1.3.1 The Aquaculture Ecosystem 20
- 1.3.2 Closed vs Open Systems..21
- 1.3.3 Understanding Carrying Capacity...23
- 1.3.4 Feed Conversion Ratio (FCR)...25
- 1.3.5 Sustainability in Aquaculture...27

CHAPTER 2
SETTING UP YOUR SHRIMP FARM 28

2.1 Choosing the Right Location 28
- 2.1.1 Factors to Consider...29
- 2.1.2 Water Source...30
- 2.1.3 Land Topography...31
- 2.1.4 Proximity to Markets...33
- 2.1.5 Regulatory and Environmental Considerations 34

2.2 Indoor vs Outdoor Farming: Pros and Cons 35
- 2.2.1 Outdoor Shrimp Farming...36
- 2.2.2 Indoor Shrimp Farming..39
- 2.2.3 Hybrid Systems 43

2.3 Designing and Building Shrimp Ponds or Tanks 44
- 2.3.1 Pond Design...45
- 2.3.2 Tank Systems for Indoor Farming..51
- 2.3.3 Recirculating Aquaculture Systems (RAS).....................................52

2.4 Water Quality Management: pH, Salinity, and Temperature 54
- 2.4.1 pH Levels 55
- 2.4.2 Salinity...57
- 2.4.3 Temperature Control 59
- 2.4.4 Dissolved Oxygen (DO) 60
- 2.4.5 Ammonia, Nitrite, and Nitrate..62
- 2.4.6 Water Testing and Monitoring...64

CHAPTER 3 66
SHRIMP HATCHERY MANAGEMENT 66

3.1 Breeding Shrimp: Setting Up a Hatchery 66
- 3.1.1 Site Selection for Hatchery 67
- 3.1.2 Hatchery Design and Infrastructure 68
- 3.1.3 Selecting Broodstock 70
- 3.1.4 Spawning Techniques 70

3.2 Larval Rearing Techniques 71
- 3.2.1 Larval Stages and Development 72
- 3.2.2 Feeding Practices 73
- 3.2.3 Water Quality Management for Larvae 74
- 3.2.4 Stocking Density and Management 76
- 3.2.5 Harvesting Post-Larvae 77

3.3 Common Hatchery Challenges and Solutions 78
- 3.3.1 Identifying Common Diseases 79
- 3.3.2 Common Problems 81
- 3.3.3 Nutritional Deficiencies 82
- 3.3.4 Environmental Stressors 84
- 3.3.5 Record Keeping and Monitoring 85

CHAPTER 4 88
FEED AND NUTRITION 88

4.1 Shrimp Nutritional Needs 88
- 4.1.1 Essential Nutrients 88
- 4.1.2 Growth Stages and Nutritional Requirements 92
- 4.1.3 Digestive Physiology of Shrimp 95

4.2 Commercial Feeds Vs Natural Feeds 97
- 4.2.1 Types of Commercial Feeds 98
- 4.2.2 Benefits and Drawbacks 101
- 4.2.3 Natural Feeds 103
- 4.2.4 Feeding Strategies 105

4.3 Feeding Schedules and Best Practices 108
- 4.3.1 Establishing Feeding Schedules 108
- 4.3.2 Feeding Methods 110
- 4.3.3 Behavioral Observations 112
- 4.3.4 Adjusting Feeding Practices 112

4.4 Enhancing Shrimp Growth and Health 114
- 4.4.1 Nutritional Supplements 114
- 4.4.2 Feeding for Stress Reduction 115
- 4.4.3 Evaluating Growth Performance 116
- 4.4.4 Research and Innovation in Shrimp Nutrition 118

CHAPTER 5 121
SHRIMP HEALTH MANAGEMENT 121

5.1 RECOGNIZING COMMON SHRIMP DISEASES 121
   5.1.1 Viral Diseases 121
   5.1.2 Bacterial Diseases 123
   5.1.3 Fungal Diseases 124
   5.1.4 Parasitic Diseases 125
5.2 PREVENTATIVE MEASURES AND HEALTH MONITORING 127
   5.2.1 Biosecurity Protocols 127
   5.2.2 Farm Hygiene and Sanitation 130
   5.2.3 Nutrition and Immunity 132
5.3 TREATMENT METHODS AND BIOSECURITY PROTOCOLS 133
   5.3.1 Disease Treatment Approaches 134
   5.3.2 Probiotic Treatments 135
   5.3.3 Vaccines and Immunostimulants 136
   5.3.4 Isolation and Containment 137

CHAPTER 6 140

WATER QUALITY AND ENVIRONMENTAL CONTROL 140

6.1 THE IMPORTANCE OF WATER QUALITY FOR SHRIMP HEALTH 140
   6.1.1 Role of Water Quality in Shrimp Physiology 140
   6.1.2 Environmental Stressors and Shrimp Health 142
   6.1.3 Economic Impacts of Poor Water Quality 144
6.2 MONITORING AND MANAGING KEY WATER PARAMETERS 146
   6.2.1 Dissolved Oxygen (DO) 146
   6.2.2 pH Levels 148
   6.2.3 Salinity 150
   6.2.4 Temperature 151
   6.2.5 Ammonia, Nitrites, and Nitrates 152
   6.2.6 Turbidity 153
   6.2.7 Alkalinity and Hardness 155
6.3 WASTE MANAGEMENT AND FILTRATION SYSTEMS 156
   6.3.1 The Role of Waste Management in Shrimp Farming 156
   6.3.2 Mechanical Filtration Systems 157
   6.3.3 Biological Filtration Systems 158
   6.3.4 Water Recirculation and Exchange Systems 159
   6.3.5 Sedimentation and Settling Ponds 159

CHAPTER 7 161

HARVESTING AND POST-HARVEST CARE 161

7.1 TIMING THE HARVEST: SIGNS OF SHRIMP READINESS 161
   7.1.1 Growth Monitoring 161
   7.1.2 Behavioral and Physical Indicators 163
   7.1.3 Environmental Considerations 164
7.2 HARVESTING TECHNIQUES FOR MAXIMUM YIELD 166
   7.2.1 Partial vs. Full Harvesting 167
   7.2.2 Drain Harvesting 168

    7.2.3 Cast Netting and Seine Netting 170
    7.2.4 Pump Harvesting 171
    7.2.5 Key Considerations for Harvesting 173
  7.3 POST-HARVEST HANDLING AND QUALITY CONTROL 174
    7.3.1 De-stressing and Resting 175
    7.3.2 Sorting and Grading 176
    7.3.3 Handling and Cleaning 178
    7.3.4 Importance of Cold Chain Management 180
    7.3.5 Quality Control and Shelf-Life Preservation.................................181
  7.4 PACKAGING AND TRANSPORT FOR MARKET 183
    7.4.1 Chilling and Freezing 183
    7.4.2 Packaging Methods..186
    7.4.3 Transport Logistics 188
    7.4.4 Minimizing Transport Time 189
    7.4.5 Market Preparation and Presentation 190
CONCLUSION 193

CHAPTER 1

INTRODUCTION TO SHRIMP FARMING

1.1 History and Evolution of Shrimp Farming

Shrimp farming has a rich history that stretches back centuries, with its roots found in the traditional aquaculture practices of Southeast Asia. In these early stages, shrimp were cultivated using simple, low-impact techniques, often in small coastal ponds or rice paddies, where shrimp would naturally thrive. These early methods were largely sustainable and relied on the natural food chains in these environments. Farmers at that time had a deep understanding of local ecosystems, which allowed them to manage shrimp production in harmony with nature. This era marked the humble beginnings of shrimp farming before it became a global industry.

1.1.1 Global Growth and Industrialization
In the 20th century, particularly during the 1970s and 1980s, shrimp farming experienced a dramatic

transformation. Technological advancements spurred the rapid growth of commercial shrimp production on a large scale, especially in regions like Latin America, Southeast Asia, and parts of the U.S. Improved scientific understanding of shrimp biology, coupled with new aquaculture techniques, paved the way for the industrialization of shrimp farming. Large-scale shrimp farms began to emerge, equipped with controlled environments that optimized growth conditions, allowed for year-round production, and greatly increased shrimp yields. The expansion of global demand for seafood, particularly in the West, further fueled this growth. Shrimp farming became a highly lucrative sector of the aquaculture industry.

1.1.2 The Role of Innovation

Innovation has been a driving force behind the success of modern shrimp farming. One key milestone was the development of hatcheries, which allowed for the controlled breeding and rearing of shrimp larvae in captivity. This breakthrough reduced the industry's dependence on wild-caught shrimp juveniles, ensuring a more reliable and consistent supply of stock. Improvements in shrimp feed formulations also played a crucial role, as new feeds were designed to meet the specific nutritional needs of shrimp at different life stages, significantly boosting growth rates and health. In parallel, advancements in disease management helped the industry tackle the challenges of pathogens that could decimate shrimp populations. Techniques such as selective breeding for disease-resistant strains, the use of probiotics, and better biosecurity measures have all contributed to reducing the risks of disease outbreaks.

1.1.3 Sustainability Concerns and Reforms

However, with rapid growth came significant challenges. The early phases of large-scale shrimp farming were marred by environmental degradation, including the destruction of critical ecosystems such as mangroves, which serve as natural buffers against coastal erosion and nurseries for marine life. The unregulated use of chemicals and antibiotics, as well as the discharge of waste and pollutants into surrounding waters, led to water pollution and long-term ecological damage. Furthermore, the industry faced scrutiny for poor labor conditions in some regions, raising ethical concerns about the treatment of workers. In response, modern shrimp farming has begun to embrace sustainability reforms aimed at mitigating these impacts. Efforts include adopting sustainable aquaculture practices, reducing chemical use, implementing better waste management systems, and seeking certifications such as the Aquaculture Stewardship Council (ASC) or GlobalG.A.P., which ensure farms meet environmental and social standards.

1.1.4 The Future of Shrimp Farming

Looking to the future, shrimp farming is poised for further innovation. One promising development is the adoption of recirculating aquaculture systems (RAS), which allow farmers to raise shrimp in controlled indoor environments, significantly reducing the industry's reliance on natural water bodies and minimizing the risk of pollution. These systems can also recycle water, making them more sustainable and eco-friendly. The idea of urban shrimp farming is also gaining traction, with shrimp farms being integrated into cities to reduce transportation costs and bring production closer to consumers. Additionally, advancements in automation and artificial intelligence are beginning to streamline farm operations, from monitoring water quality and feeding schedules to predicting disease outbreaks. These technologies are set to revolutionize shrimp farming by improving efficiency, reducing labor needs, and enhancing sustainability, ensuring that the industry can meet growing global demand without compromising the environment or ethical standards.

1.2 Overview of Shrimp Species for Farming

When it comes to shrimp farming, selecting the right species is critical to success. Several species dominate the global shrimp farming industry, each with unique traits that make them suitable for different environments and farming conditions. By understanding the strengths, growth characteristics, and farming requirements of each species, farmers can make informed decisions about which shrimp to raise based on their location, climate, and market demands.

1.2.1 Whiteleg Shrimp (Litopenaeus vannamei)

One of the most commonly farmed species is the Whiteleg Shrimp (Litopenaeus vannamei), also known as the Pacific white shrimp. Native to the eastern Pacific Ocean, this species has become a staple in shrimp farming due to its numerous advantages. Whiteleg shrimp grow rapidly, reaching market size in as little as three to four months, depending on the farming conditions. They are highly adaptable to a wide range of environments, thriving in both saline and brackish water, and they can tolerate fluctuations in water quality better than many other species. Additionally, this species has been selectively bred for disease resistance, further boosting its popularity among farmers. The fast growth, adaptability, and disease resistance make the Whiteleg shrimp the preferred choice for many commercial shrimp farms, particularly in tropical and subtropical regions like Latin America, Southeast Asia, and parts of the United States.

1.2.2 Giant Tiger Prawn (Penaeus monodon)
Another prominent species in the shrimp farming industry is the Giant Tiger Prawn (Penaeus monodon), known for its impressive size and high

market value. This species is particularly popular in Asia, where it has been farmed for decades. Giant tiger prawns are much larger than whiteleg shrimp, with some individuals reaching lengths of over 30 cm. Their large size makes them a sought-after product in premium seafood markets, where they command higher prices. However, farming giant tiger prawns presents more challenges than whiteleg shrimp. They require specific environmental conditions, such as higher salinity levels and warmer temperatures, to thrive. They are also more susceptible to certain diseases, making them a bit more labor-intensive and expensive to raise. Despite these challenges, the species' high market demand and profitability keep it as a key player in the industry.

1.2.3 Other Species

In addition to these two species, there are several other shrimp that, while less commonly farmed, have important roles in niche markets or in certain regions.

The **Kuruma Prawn (Marsupenaeus japonicus),** native to the Indo-Pacific region, is prized for its high quality and flavor, particularly in Japan. Kuruma prawns require precise farming conditions and are often raised in highly controlled environments, which makes them less common but highly valuable. The **Northern White Shrimp (Litopenaeus setiferus),** native to the Atlantic coast of the United States, is another species that has seen some success in aquaculture, especially in North America. Unlike most of the popular shrimp species, **Caridean shrimp**—a group of freshwater shrimp species—offer an alternative for farming in inland areas, particularly in freshwater ponds or tanks, making them an option for farmers without access to coastal or brackish waters.

1.2.3 Species Selection Based on Location
When choosing which species to farm, one of the primary considerations is location. The climate, water

temperature, and salinity levels of a given area heavily influence the suitability of different shrimp species. For example, Whiteleg shrimp are well-suited to tropical and subtropical climates, where warm temperatures and brackish waters mimic their natural habitat. This species can tolerate lower salinity, making it ideal for farmers who do not have access to highly saline water sources. On the other hand, Giant Tiger Prawns are better suited to areas with higher salinity levels and more stable, warm climates, as they require specific water conditions to thrive. In temperate regions, farming shrimp can be more challenging due to cooler temperatures, but some farmers have successfully raised Northern White Shrimp or used recirculating aquaculture systems (RAS) to maintain the necessary water temperatures.

1.2.4 Growth Rates and Yields

Growth rates and yields also vary significantly between species. Whiteleg shrimp are known for their fast growth, often reaching market size (15-20 grams) in just three to four months, with survival rates generally ranging from 70% to 90% under optimal conditions. This allows farmers to harvest multiple crops per year. Giant Tiger Prawns, on the other hand, take longer to grow, often requiring five to six months to reach market size due to their larger size. However, their higher market value compensates for the longer growth period. The yields for these species can vary depending on stocking density, water quality, and management practices, but generally, whiteleg shrimp farms can achieve higher yields per hectare due to the species' faster growth and higher stocking densities.

1.2.5 Choosing the Right Species for Beginners

For newcomers to the shrimp farming industry, selecting the right species is crucial for early success. **Whiteleg shrimp** are often considered the best option for beginners due to their **adaptability, fast growth rates**, and **relative ease of farming**. They are more **resilient to environmental fluctuations** and **diseases** compared to other species, making them less risky for farmers with less experience. Additionally, their **short production cycle** allows new farmers to quickly see the results of their efforts, which can be encouraging for those just starting out. In contrast, ***Giant Tiger Prawns***, while highly ***profitable,*** are more sensitive to environmental conditions and require ***more advanced management techniques***, which may make them more suitable for experienced farmers.

1.3 Key Concepts in Aquaculture

Aquaculture, the cultivation of aquatic organisms such as fish, crustaceans, and plants, is a rapidly growing sector of global food production. It encompasses a wide range of practices aimed at raising these organisms in controlled or semi-controlled environments to meet the increasing demand for seafood and other aquatic products. Shrimp farming is a major component of aquaculture, specifically focusing on the cultivation of shrimp for commercial purposes. This form of aquaculture plays a significant role in feeding populations worldwide and providing livelihoods to millions of people, particularly in coastal regions.

1.3.1 The Aquaculture Ecosystem

At the heart of any shrimp farming operation is the aquaculture ecosystem, where there is a dynamic interaction between shrimp, their environment, and the farmer. Shrimp are raised in water environments where the quality of that water is crucial for their health and growth. One key concept in managing this ecosystem is the nitrogen cycle, which describes how nitrogen, often introduced through shrimp waste and uneaten feed, is broken down into less harmful compounds by bacteria. These bacteria convert ammonia (a toxic byproduct) into nitrites and eventually nitrates, which are less harmful but can accumulate to dangerous levels if not managed. Farmers must monitor water quality parameters such as pH, temperature, and dissolved oxygen levels to ensure the environment remains suitable for shrimp. Water quality management involves maintaining a balance between these factors, adjusting feeding practices, aeration, and water exchange to create optimal conditions for shrimp to thrive.

1.3.2 Closed vs Open Systems

Shrimp farms can be classified into open systems and closed systems, each with its own advantages and challenges. **Open systems** include **ponds or coastal** areas where shrimp are raised in water directly connected to natural water bodies, such as the **ocean or estuaries**. These systems tend to be less expensive to establish and operate, as they rely on natural water flow and conditions. However, open systems are also more vulnerable to environmental changes, such as pollution, temperature fluctuations, and disease outbreaks, which can be introduced from the surrounding environment. Additionally, they may have a greater impact on local ecosystems, as waste and chemicals from the farm can contaminate nearby waters. In contrast, **closed systems**, such as **land-based tanks or indoor** farming facilities, provide a much higher level of control over the farming environment. In these systems, water is often recirculated and treated, allowing farmers to maintain stable conditions and reduce the risk of introducing external contaminants. Closed systems also have a lower environmental footprint, as they minimize water usage and prevent the release of pollutants into natural water bodies. However, they come with higher costs for setup, maintenance, and energy use, and managing water quality in such systems can be technically demanding. Closed systems are generally considered more sustainable but may be less scalable due to these increased costs.

1.3.3 Understanding Carrying Capacity

A key concept in aquaculture is carrying capacity, which refers to the maximum number of shrimp that can be sustainably farmed in a given space without negatively impacting their health or the environment. Carrying capacity is determined by several factors, including water quality, available oxygen, waste buildup, and the ability of the system to maintain these conditions over time. Exceeding the carrying capacity can lead to poor water quality, increased stress, and higher susceptibility to diseases, ultimately reducing the productivity of the farm. Farmers must carefully monitor their systems and adjust factors such as aeration, filtration, and feeding to ensure the system remains within its carrying capacity.

Closely related to carrying capacity is stocking density, which refers to the number of shrimp stocked per square meter of pond or tank space. Stocking density is a critical factor that affects both the growth rates and the overall health of the shrimp. If too many shrimp are stocked in a given space, competition for oxygen and food increases, stress levels rise, and the likelihood of disease outbreaks grows. Conversely, if stocking densities are too low, the farm may not be operating at its full potential, resulting in lower yields. The optimal stocking density varies depending on the species being farmed, the farming system used, and the goals of the operation. Intensive systems, such as those found in indoor tanks with sophisticated water treatment systems, can support much higher stocking densities than extensive systems, like earthen ponds, where shrimp are more reliant on natural conditions.

1.3.4 Feed Conversion Ratio (FCR)

One of the most important metrics in aquaculture is the Feed Conversion Ratio (FCR), which measures how efficiently shrimp convert feed into body mass. An FCR of 1.5, for example, means that 1.5 kilograms of feed are required to produce 1 kilogram of shrimp. Improving FCR is critical for reducing costs and improving the profitability of shrimp farming operations. Farmers can optimize FCR by using high-quality, nutritionally balanced feeds, ensuring that shrimp are fed in appropriate quantities and at the right times, and maintaining optimal water quality. Overfeeding can lead to wasted feed, poor water quality, and increased costs, while underfeeding can stunt growth and reduce yields. Automated feeding systems and careful monitoring of shrimp feeding behavior are increasingly used to ensure the most efficient use of feed.

Another crucial element in successful shrimp farming is biosecurity—the practices put in place to prevent the introduction and spread of diseases, which can devastate shrimp populations and cause significant financial losses. Disease outbreaks are one of the biggest risks in aquaculture, and biosecurity measures are essential to minimizing this threat. Basic principles of biosecurity include controlling access to the farm, ensuring that water is properly filtered and treated, and monitoring shrimp health closely for early signs of disease. Quarantine practices, where new or sick shrimp are isolated from the rest of the stock, are also important in preventing the spread of pathogens. Farmers often rely on regular water testing, vaccination programs, and the use of probiotics to promote a healthy environment and reduce the need for antibiotics or chemicals.

1.3.5 Sustainability in Aquaculture

Finally, sustainability in aquaculture is a growing concern as the demand for farmed shrimp continues to rise. Shrimp farming has historically been associated with negative environmental impacts, such as the destruction of mangrove forests, water pollution, and the overuse of chemicals and antibiotics. Modern shrimp farming practices increasingly emphasize sustainability, focusing on reducing these negative impacts while maintaining high productivity. Responsible farming practices include using recirculating aquaculture systems (RAS) to minimize water usage, employing biological filtration systems to reduce chemical use, and adopting integrated multi-trophic aquaculture (IMTA) systems, where shrimp are farmed alongside other species, such as algae or shellfish, to create a balanced ecosystem that naturally processes waste. Certifications, such as the Aquaculture Stewardship

Council (ASC) or GlobalG.A.P., provide assurance that farms are following best practices in sustainability, including protecting natural habitats, reducing the carbon footprint of production, and ensuring fair labor practices.

CHAPTER 2

SETTING UP YOUR SHRIMP FARM

2.1 Choosing the Right Location

Choosing the right location for a shrimp farm is a foundational decision that directly affects the success, sustainability, and profitability of the venture. The location you choose will influence everything from water quality and availability to operational costs and environmental impact. A thorough evaluation of several critical factors is essential when selecting a site for shrimp farming.

2.1.1 Factors to Consider

One of the most important factors to consider is the climate of the area. Shrimp are ectothermic animals, meaning their growth and metabolic processes are highly influenced by the surrounding water temperature. Warmer climates generally provide the most favorable conditions for shrimp farming because they support year-round growth and allow for multiple harvests within a single year. Tropical and subtropical regions, where temperatures stay relatively stable throughout the year, are ideal for outdoor shrimp ponds. In contrast, colder regions may experience significant seasonal fluctuations that can slow down shrimp growth or even halt production during colder months. Farmers in these regions may need to invest in indoor systems with controlled temperature settings or use heating systems to maintain optimal conditions. Understanding how seasonal changes in temperature affect shrimp growth and metabolism is crucial, as extreme temperatures—both too high and too low—can cause stress or mortality in shrimp.

2.1.2 Water Source

Another key consideration is the availability and quality of the water source. Shrimp farming is a water-intensive activity, so it is essential to have a reliable and abundant supply of clean water. The type of water source—whether it is freshwater, seawater, or even brackish water—depends on the species of shrimp being farmed. Whiteleg shrimp (Litopenaeus vannamei), for example, are highly adaptable and can thrive in both freshwater and low-salinity environments, whereas species like the giant tiger prawn (Penaeus monodon) prefer higher salinities. Farmers should assess the proximity of natural water bodies, such as rivers, lakes, or coastal waters, and the possibility of using groundwater if necessary. The quality of the water is equally important, as shrimp are highly sensitive to pollutants and toxins. Contaminated water sources can lead to disease outbreaks, poor growth rates, and increased mortality. It is essential to conduct water quality tests to check for contaminants, such as heavy metals, pesticides, and harmful bacteria, before establishing the farm. Additionally, farmers should ensure that the water source is sustainable and available year-round to avoid disruptions in production.

2.1.3 Land Topography

Land topography is another important factor in selecting the right location for a shrimp farm. Flat, low-lying areas near coastal regions or estuaries are ideal for outdoor shrimp ponds. These areas naturally facilitate water flow and drainage, reducing the need for extensive engineering or construction work. Coastal areas provide easy access to seawater, making them suitable for farming marine shrimp species. However, the proximity to the coast also requires consideration of the risk of flooding, saltwater intrusion, and storm surges. Therefore, farms located near coastal zones should be designed with protective measures, such as levees or drainage systems, to mitigate these risks. On the other hand, sloped or hilly areas are generally less favorable because they require additional infrastructure, such as pumps, to move water uphill, which can increase operational costs. In some cases, terracing or leveling the land may be necessary, adding to the initial investment required to prepare the site. Therefore, the physical characteristics of the land should be closely examined to determine the most cost-effective and efficient way to set up the shrimp farming operation.

2.1.4 Proximity to Markets

Proximity to markets is another critical factor when choosing a shrimp farm location. Shrimp are a highly perishable product, and their quality begins to decline soon after harvesting. Being close to processing facilities, transportation hubs, and markets allows for faster delivery times and better product quality, as it reduces the risk of spoilage and extends the shelf life of the shrimp. Transportation infrastructure, such as access to roads, ports, or airports, should be evaluated to ensure efficient logistics for both the farm's inputs (e.g., feed, equipment, and supplies) and its outputs (harvested shrimp). Additionally, proximity to processing plants can reduce costs associated with transportation, cold storage, and handling. Farms located far from markets may incur higher operational costs and face challenges in delivering fresh shrimp to consumers or export markets. Therefore, shrimp farmers should carefully assess how their location will affect the logistics of their supply chain and the cost-effectiveness of their operations.

2.1.5 Regulatory and Environmental Considerations

In addition to physical and logistical considerations, regulatory and environmental factors play a crucial role in determining the suitability of a location for shrimp farming. Farmers must ensure that their operations comply with local, national, and international regulations, which often include environmental impact assessments, zoning laws, and permits for water use or construction. The shrimp farming industry has come under scrutiny in many regions for its environmental impact, particularly in terms of habitat destruction (such as mangrove deforestation), water pollution, and overuse of chemicals. Before selecting a site, farmers must conduct an environmental impact assessment to determine the potential effects of the farm on the local ecosystem and biodiversity. This process helps identify any potential risks, such as harm to wetlands, wildlife habitats, or water sources, and offers strategies to mitigate those risks. In many countries, obtaining permits for shrimp farming involves demonstrating compliance with sustainability standards, such as using recirculating aquaculture systems (RAS), implementing biosecurity measures, and adhering to responsible farming practices. Additionally, some regions have specific zoning laws that regulate where shrimp farms can be established, often limiting operations to certain coastal or rural areas to prevent urban encroachment.

2.2 Indoor vs Outdoor Farming: Pros and Cons

When deciding between indoor and outdoor shrimp farming, each approach has distinct advantages and challenges that affect factors such as infrastructure costs, environmental control, and production consistency. The decision largely depends on the farm's location, available resources, and the goals of the farmer. A detailed comparison of both methods highlights their respective pros and cons, helping farmers make informed choices based on their specific needs and circumstances.

2.2.1 Outdoor Shrimp Farming

Outdoor shrimp farming has long been the traditional method, particularly in coastal and rural areas with access to natural water bodies like estuaries, rivers, or the ocean. This approach leverages the natural environment, making it an attractive option for many farmers due to its lower setup costs and simpler infrastructure requirements.

One of the major advantages of outdoor farming is that shrimp can benefit from natural sunlight, which promotes healthier growth and supports the development of their immune systems. Exposure to sunlight also enhances the natural production of algae and plankton in the water, which can supplement shrimp feed and reduce feeding costs. Additionally, the ecosystem services provided by natural ponds or water bodies—such as natural aeration and water filtration through biological processes—can lower the complexity and cost of water management. Another advantage is the lower upfront costs associated with outdoor systems. Farmers do not need to invest in expensive indoor infrastructure, such as tanks, climate control systems, or advanced water filtration technologies. The ability to use natural water bodies can also reduce the need for extensive water treatment systems, allowing farmers to harness local resources more efficiently. In many regions, particularly in tropical and subtropical climates, shrimp can be farmed outdoors year-round, leading to multiple harvests without the need for artificial environmental control. However, outdoor shrimp farming comes with significant challenges. The most prominent is the farm's vulnerability to weather changes. Storms, floods, and temperature fluctuations can all disrupt production and lead to significant shrimp losses. For example, sudden drops in water temperature during cold fronts can stress the shrimp, weakening their immune systems and making them more susceptible to diseases. Likewise, heavy rainfall can dilute water salinity levels, which is critical for the health of many shrimp species, especially marine species that require specific salinity ranges.

Another challenge is the greater exposure to diseases and environmental contaminants. Outdoor systems are more susceptible to disease outbreaks, as they are open to interaction with wild animals, including birds, fish, and other aquatic species that may carry pathogens. Contaminated water from nearby agricultural runoff, industrial pollution, or human activity can introduce toxins or harmful microorganisms into shrimp ponds, affecting the health and survival rates of the shrimp. Additionally, outdoor shrimp farms have the potential to cause significant environmental impacts if not managed responsibly. Waste, such as excess feed, shrimp excrement, and chemicals, can accumulate in the water, leading to nutrient pollution, eutrophication, and damage to local ecosystems, including nearby wetlands or coastal areas. Poor waste management can also contribute to the depletion of oxygen levels in the water, creating hypoxic conditions that harm shrimp and other aquatic life. To mitigate these impacts, farmers need to implement effective waste treatment and water filtration systems, which can add to operational costs.

2.2.2 Indoor Shrimp Farming
Indoor shrimp farming represents a more controlled and technologically advanced approach, offering greater precision in managing environmental conditions. It is especially popular in regions where

outdoor farming is less feasible due to climate or environmental concerns.

One of the key advantages of indoor shrimp farming is the complete control over the farming environment. Farmers can regulate crucial factors such as temperature, water quality, lighting, and salinity. This level of control minimizes the impact of external weather conditions, ensuring a stable and consistent environment for shrimp to grow. For example, indoor systems can maintain optimal temperatures year-round, allowing for continuous production even in regions with cold winters. Indoor farms are also equipped with sophisticated filtration systems that allow for precise control of water parameters, which can result in higher survival and growth rates for shrimp. Another advantage is the reduced risk of disease and environmental contamination. By operating in a closed system, indoor farms are isolated from external pathogens and pollutants that could be introduced from wild animals or contaminated water sources. This biosecurity advantage significantly reduces the likelihood of disease outbreaks, which is a common concern in outdoor systems. Moreover, indoor farms often have strict biosecurity protocols, such as controlled access to facilities, water filtration, and the use of disinfectants to minimize disease risk.

Indoor systems are also known for their more efficient water use and waste management. Most indoor farms use recirculating aquaculture systems (RAS), which recycle water and treat it through filtration systems to remove waste products. This not only reduces water consumption but also minimizes the environmental impact by preventing the discharge of pollutants into natural ecosystems. RAS technology also allows farmers to optimize water quality by continuously monitoring parameters such as pH, ammonia levels, and oxygen concentration, ensuring that the shrimp have ideal growing conditions. However, indoor shrimp farming has several challenges, primarily related to its higher initial setup and operating costs. The infrastructure needed for indoor farming—including tanks, filtration systems, heating or cooling units, and advanced monitoring equipment—can require significant upfront investment. Additionally, the ongoing costs of energy, equipment maintenance, and water treatment are higher than in outdoor systems. For instance, maintaining a controlled environment requires constant electricity for lighting, temperature regulation, and water filtration, which can increase operational expenses.

Another challenge is the limited space available in indoor farms. While indoor systems are more efficient in terms of water use and waste management, they are often confined to relatively small areas, which can limit the scale of production. Expanding an indoor farm requires additional investment in infrastructure and technology, which may not always be feasible for smaller operators. Additionally, indoor systems demand more expertise in technology and monitoring systems. Farmers must be well-versed in the operation of complex equipment and be able to respond to technical issues, such as system malfunctions or water quality fluctuations, in real time.

2.2.3 Hybrid Systems
Some farmers have adopted hybrid systems that combine elements of both indoor and outdoor shrimp farming. These systems aim to balance the lower costs and natural benefits of outdoor farming with the environmental control and biosecurity advantages of indoor systems. For example, farmers may use outdoor ponds with sophisticated water control

systems to manage salinity, oxygen levels, and temperature more precisely. Alternatively, semi-enclosed environments can protect the shrimp from extreme weather and predators while still benefiting from natural sunlight and water sources. Hybrid systems offer a middle ground, allowing farmers to reduce costs while maintaining better control over environmental factors and improving biosecurity. These systems can be particularly useful in regions where outdoor farming is viable but requires additional management to mitigate risks such as disease or pollution.

2.3 Designing and Building Shrimp Ponds or Tanks

Designing and building effective shrimp ponds or tanks is a crucial step in ensuring the success of a shrimp farming operation. The design of these systems influences water quality, shrimp health, and the efficiency of day-to-day operations.

Understanding the different design options and their impact on productivity helps farmers select the best setup for their environment, budget, and production goals.

2.3.1 Pond Design

Shrimp farming in outdoor ponds has been a popular choice due to its relatively low costs and scalability. However, designing the right pond is essential for ensuring water quality, shrimp welfare, and ease of management.

Types of Ponds

There are several types of shrimp ponds, each with distinct benefits and trade-offs. Earthen ponds are the most traditional and cost-effective type. They are dug into the ground, with soil or clay serving as the natural lining. These ponds can be easily constructed but require ongoing maintenance to prevent erosion, seepage, and the accumulation of organic waste at the pond bottom. They are best suited for farmers in coastal regions with access to natural water sources and minimal infrastructure. **Concrete-lined ponds** are more durable and easier to clean than earthen ponds, but they come with higher construction costs. The smooth surfaces prevent waste and sediment buildup, making them easier to manage and ideal for high-intensity shrimp farming. Plastic-lined ponds offer a middle ground, providing better water retention and reducing the risk of erosion compared to earthen ponds. They are less expensive than concrete but may require replacement after several years of use, depending on the quality of the liner material. When selecting the type of pond, farmers must weigh the initial investment against the long-term maintenance and operational costs. For smaller-scale farms or those in regions with poor soil conditions, lined ponds may be a better option.

Size and Shape

The size and shape of shrimp ponds directly affect their management and efficiency. While pond size can vary widely depending on the scale of the operation, typical shrimp ponds range from 0.5 to 5 hectares. Larger ponds offer the advantage of greater production capacity, but they also pose more challenges in terms of water quality management and aeration. Smaller ponds, on the other hand, allow for easier control of water parameters and may be more suitable for farms in areas with limited space or water resources. The shape of the pond plays a role in water flow and shrimp harvesting efficiency. Rectangular ponds are commonly used because they are easier to manage in terms of aeration and harvesting. Paddlewheel aerators, for example, can be placed at the pond's edges, promoting efficient oxygen distribution and circulation. Circular ponds, while less common, offer superior water circulation and can reduce the buildup of waste and debris in stagnant areas, as the circular motion naturally drives particles towards a central drainage point. Farmers should aim for a pond shape that maximizes water movement and aeration, ensuring even distribution of oxygen and preventing the formation of dead zones where water quality could deteriorate.

Depth Considerations

Pond depth is another critical factor that affects shrimp growth, water temperature, and oxygen levels. Shrimp ponds are typically designed to have a depth of 1 to 2 meters, which is optimal for maintaining stable water temperatures and good oxygenation throughout the water column. Shallow ponds (less than 1-meter-deep) can lead to excessive temperature fluctuations and oxygen depletion, especially during hot weather, which can stress the shrimp and slow their growth. Deeper ponds, on the other hand, may have areas with low oxygen levels at the bottom due to poor water circulation. To mitigate this, farmers must ensure that the pond's aeration system is robust enough to circulate water from top to bottom, maintaining a consistent environment for shrimp throughout the pond.

Drainage and Water Inflow Systems

A well-designed drainage system is essential for managing water quality and preventing problems like stagnation or flooding. Ponds should be equipped with both inflow and outflow systems to allow for regular water exchange, which is critical for removing waste, regulating salinity, and maintaining optimal water quality.

Gravity-fed drainage systems are commonly used in outdoor ponds, taking advantage of the natural slope of the land to move water in and out without the need for pumps. Pump-driven systems, while more expensive, offer greater control over water exchange and can be used in areas where gravity flow is not feasible, such as in flat or low-lying regions. In both cases, it is important to design the pond with a slight slope (typically 1-2%) to ensure that water can flow freely towards the drainage point. Proper slope design helps prevent the buildup of waste at the bottom of the pond and makes it easier to fully drain the pond when necessary for cleaning or harvesting.

Slope and Pond Liners

The slope of a shrimp pond is essential for effective water flow and waste management. As water circulates within the pond, it naturally moves waste and debris toward the drain, where it can be removed from the system. A pond slope of 1-2% is ideal for promoting this flow while ensuring that the pond remains stable and that water does not erode the pond banks. Using pond liners can further improve water quality and reduce seepage, which is especially important in regions with porous or sandy soils. Liners also help prevent the loss of valuable water and minimize the risk of contamination from the surrounding environment. While more expensive than natural earthen ponds, liners provide long-term benefits by simplifying pond management and reducing maintenance costs.

2.3.2 Tank Systems for Indoor Farming

Indoor shrimp farming requires a different approach, with tanks replacing the open-air ponds used in outdoor systems. Tanks provide greater environmental control and are essential for farms in regions with extreme weather or limited access to natural water bodies.

Types of Tanks

Indoor shrimp farming systems can use a variety of tank materials and designs, depending on the scale of the operation and the farmer's budget. Fiberglass tanks are commonly used because they are lightweight, durable, and easy to clean. Plastic tanks are another popular option, offering affordability and flexibility in design. Concrete tanks, while more expensive, provide long-term durability and are often used in large-scale operations. In terms of shape, round tanks are often favored because they promote better water circulation, which is important for maintaining water quality. Rectangular tanks, however, are easier to fit into available space and may be more practical for smaller indoor farms. Modular or prefabricated tanks offer additional advantages, as they can be easily transported, assembled, and expanded as the farm grows.

2.3.3 Recirculating Aquaculture Systems (RAS)

A key feature of many indoor farming operations is the use of Recirculating Aquaculture Systems (RAS), which continuously filter and recirculate water within the system. RAS technology significantly reduces water usage and allows for precise control of water parameters, such as temperature, pH, and oxygen levels. In a RAS setup, water passes through mechanical and biological filtration systems to remove waste, nitrogen compounds, and toxins before being returned to the tanks. This process allows farmers to maintain a stable and healthy environment for shrimp while minimizing the environmental impact of water discharge.

Aeration and Filtration

Proper aeration and filtration are critical to the success of both pond and tank-based shrimp farming. Aeration ensures that there is sufficient oxygen in the water for shrimp to thrive, while filtration removes harmful waste products that can accumulate over time. In outdoor ponds, paddlewheels are often used to aerate the water by creating surface agitation and promoting gas exchange. For indoor systems, air diffusers or blowers may be used to introduce oxygen directly into the water, ensuring that it is evenly distributed throughout the tank.

Filtration systems are equally important, as they help maintain water quality by removing waste and excess nutrients. Mechanical filtration removes large particles from the water, such as uneaten feed and shrimp excrement, while biological filtration uses beneficial bacteria to break down harmful nitrogen compounds, such as ammonia and nitrites, into less toxic forms like nitrates. A well-designed filtration system not only keeps the water clean but also supports faster growth and higher survival rates for shrimp.

2.4 Water Quality Management: pH, Salinity, and Temperature

Maintaining optimal water quality is essential for the health, growth, and survival of shrimp. Shrimp are sensitive to changes in their environment, and even small fluctuations in water parameters can cause stress, increase their susceptibility to diseases, and slow down growth rates. Poor water quality can result in lower yields and higher mortality rates, making water quality management one of the most critical aspects of shrimp farming. Farmers must consistently monitor and adjust key parameters, such as pH, salinity, temperature, dissolved oxygen, and nitrogen compounds, to create an ideal environment for shrimp. To ensure the success of a shrimp farming operation, it's important to closely monitor and control specific water parameters that directly influence shrimp health and growth.

2.4.1 pH Levels
- **Ideal pH Range:** The ideal pH range for shrimp farming is generally between 7.5 and 8.5, though it can vary slightly depending on the shrimp species. Maintaining a stable pH within this range helps optimize metabolic processes, immune function, and growth.
- **Impact of pH Fluctuations:** When pH levels are too high or too low, shrimp can experience stress, leading to reduced feeding and slower growth. At extremely high pH levels, ammonia becomes more toxic, causing shrimp to become lethargic and making them more vulnerable to diseases. On the other hand, when pH drops too low, shrimp may have difficulty molting, which can also increase mortality rates.

- **Monitoring and Adjusting pH Levels:** To maintain the ideal pH level, shrimp farmers should regularly test water pH using a pH meter or test kit. If the pH is too low, it can be adjusted by adding calcium carbonate (lime) or sodium bicarbonate to raise alkalinity. If the pH is too high, vinegar or muriatic acid can be added to lower it, though these treatments should be applied carefully and incrementally to avoid sudden shifts that could shock the shrimp. Natural additives, such as using crushed coral in filtration systems, can also help stabilize pH over time.

2.4.2 Salinity

- **Salinity Requirements:** Different shrimp species have different salinity preferences. For example, Whiteleg shrimp (Litopenaeus vannamei) thrive in salinities between 15-30 parts per thousand (ppt), while Tiger shrimp (Penaeus monodon) prefer salinities between 20-35 ppt. Maintaining the correct salinity is crucial because shrimp use osmoregulation to balance the salt and water in their bodies. Incorrect salinity can lead to stress, impaired immune function, and disruption in molting cycles.

- **Adjusting Salinity in Coastal and Inland Farms:** In coastal farms, where seawater is readily available, farmers may need to periodically adjust salinity by mixing in freshwater during dry seasons or when salinity levels rise due to evaporation. For inland farms, where freshwater or brackish water is used, adding sea salt or specific commercial salts to the water can help achieve the desired salinity levels. Care should be taken to mix the water thoroughly to ensure even distribution of salts and maintain a consistent environment for the shrimp.

- **Impact of Salinity Fluctuations:** Sudden changes in salinity can affect shrimp metabolism, molting cycles, and overall health. Fluctuating salinity levels force shrimp to expend more energy on osmoregulation, leaving them with less energy for growth and immune function. Therefore, it is important to monitor salinity frequently and avoid rapid changes by adjusting water gradually.

2.4.3 Temperature Control

- **Ideal Water Temperature:** The ideal temperature for most shrimp species is between 26-30°C (78-86°F). Temperature plays a critical role in shrimp growth rates, immune function, and metabolism. Within this temperature range, shrimp exhibit optimal feeding behavior and grow faster.

- **Impact of Temperature Fluctuations:** Temperatures below the optimal range can slow down shrimp metabolism, making them eat less and grow more slowly. In extreme cases, temperature drops can increase mortality rates by weakening the shrimp's immune response. On the other hand, temperatures that are too high can reduce dissolved oxygen levels in the water, increase stress, and contribute to disease outbreaks.

- **Practical Solutions for Temperature Control:** In outdoor ponds, temperature control can be achieved by selecting farming locations with favorable climates or by using pond covers to reduce temperature fluctuations. In indoor systems, water heaters can be used to maintain consistent temperatures. Tank insulation and proper ventilation also help regulate temperature, particularly in regions with extreme weather conditions. Some farms utilize solar heating systems or geothermal energy to reduce energy costs associated with temperature regulation.

2.4.4 Dissolved Oxygen (DO)

- **Importance of Dissolved Oxygen:** Shrimp require sufficient oxygen for respiration and overall health. The ideal dissolved oxygen (DO) level for shrimp farming is between 5-6 mg/L. Maintaining these levels ensures that shrimp can grow and thrive without stress. Low DO levels can lead to hypoxia (oxygen deficiency), which causes shrimp to become sluggish, reduces their growth, and can lead to mass mortality in extreme cases.

- **Aeration Systems:** Aeration systems are essential in both pond and tank setups, particularly in high-density farming environments. Paddlewheel aerators are commonly used in outdoor ponds to increase surface agitation and promote oxygen exchange. Diffused aeration systems or air blowers are often employed in indoor tanks to evenly distribute oxygen throughout the water column. These systems also help maintain water circulation, preventing the buildup of waste and ensuring better water quality.

- **Troubleshooting Low Oxygen:** If DO levels fall below the recommended range, several measures can be taken. These include increasing aeration, reducing the stocking density, or improving water circulation. In some cases, partial water changes may also help restore oxygen levels, particularly if the water is rich in organic matter or waste.

2.4.5 Ammonia, Nitrite, and Nitrate

- **The Nitrogen Cycle:** Shrimp farming systems produce ammonia as a natural byproduct of shrimp waste and uneaten feed. Ammonia is highly toxic to shrimp, especially when pH levels are high. The nitrogen cycle plays a crucial role in converting ammonia into less harmful substances. Beneficial bacteria convert ammonia into nitrite (which is also toxic), and then further into nitrate, which is relatively harmless at low concentrations.

- **Managing Ammonia Levels:** High ammonia levels can cause gill damage, leading to respiratory distress and increasing shrimp mortality rates. It is essential to regularly monitor ammonia using water test kits. The introduction of biological filtration systems—such as biofilters that house nitrifying bacteria—helps to convert ammonia into nitrate. In outdoor ponds, water exchange and planting aquatic vegetation can also help reduce ammonia levels by absorbing nitrogen compounds.

- **Controlling Nitrite and Nitrate:** Nitrite, like ammonia, is toxic to shrimp and must be managed carefully. Biological filtration is the primary method of converting nitrite into nitrate. However, nitrate, while less harmful, can still cause issues if it accumulates. In high-density systems, performing regular water changes or adding denitrifying bacteria can help control nitrate levels and prevent toxicity.

2.4.6 Water Testing and Monitoring

- **Importance of Regular Monitoring:** Frequent testing of water parameters is critical to maintain a healthy environment for shrimp. Farmers should monitor pH, salinity, temperature, dissolved oxygen, ammonia, nitrite, and nitrate levels regularly to detect any deviations from the optimal range.

- **Tools for Water Quality Monitoring:** Digital meters and test kits are essential tools for monitoring water quality. For example, pH meters, salinity refractometers, and dissolved oxygen meters provide accurate real-time readings. Automatic sensors and data loggers can offer continuous monitoring and can be set to alert farmers if any parameter falls outside the desired range.

- **Setting up a Monitoring Routine:** Farmers should establish a regular monitoring schedule, testing key parameters daily or weekly, depending on the system's complexity. Detailed records should be kept to track trends over time, which can help identify potential issues before they become problematic. By maintaining consistent water quality, shrimp farmers can significantly reduce stress and disease outbreaks, ensuring higher yields and healthier shrimp populations.

CHAPTER 3

SHRIMP HATCHERY MANAGEMENT

3.1 Breeding Shrimp: Setting Up a Hatchery

In shrimp farming, the hatchery plays a fundamental role as the starting point for the entire production process. It is in the hatchery that shrimp broodstock are bred and post-larvae (PL) shrimp are produced, which are then transferred to grow-out systems for maturation. Breeding your own shrimp in a hatchery offers significant advantages to farmers. Not only does it reduce reliance on external suppliers for post-larvae, but it also offers greater control over the genetic quality of the stock, allowing farmers to select broodstock with desired traits such as faster growth rates, disease resistance, and higher survival rates. Additionally, by producing shrimp in-house, farmers can more closely monitor health conditions, minimizing the risk of introducing pathogens from outside sources.

3.1.1 Site Selection for Hatchery

Choosing the right site for a shrimp hatchery is critical for ensuring the health and survival of shrimp larvae. A location with access to clean, high-quality seawater or freshwater is essential, as water quality directly affects shrimp development and overall health. The selected water source must be free from contaminants and pathogens, making it suitable for breeding and larval rearing. Along with water quality, the space available for hatchery operations must be sufficient to accommodate breeding tanks, larval rearing systems, nursery areas, and equipment storage. This ensures smooth workflow and maintenance of hatchery operations. Proximity to grow-out facilities is another key factor. Hatcheries that are located near the grow-out systems can minimize transportation stress on the post-larvae, leading to better survival rates during the transfer process.

3.1.2 Hatchery Design and Infrastructure

When it comes to hatchery design and infrastructure, proper planning is essential to maximize productivity and ensure shrimp health. The tank setup for the hatchery should include various systems designed for specific stages, such as circular tanks for broodstock, larval rearing tanks, and nursery tanks for post-larvae development. These tanks can be made from materials such as fiberglass or concrete, which are durable and resistant to corrosion. Tank size should be tailored to the needs of the shrimp species being bred and the scale of production. Aeration and water circulation systems are crucial to maintaining oxygen levels and ensuring that water quality remains consistent throughout the hatchery. Aeration helps to prevent sediment buildup and stagnation, while water circulation systems distribute heat, oxygen, and nutrients evenly within the tanks, promoting healthier shrimp growth.

Both lighting and temperature control are vital to the success of breeding operations in a hatchery. Proper lighting, known as the photoperiod, is important for regulating shrimp spawning cycles, while maintaining a stable temperature ensures optimal breeding and larval development conditions. This is particularly important in indoor hatcheries where environmental factors need to be controlled manually. The use of water heaters, chillers, and regulated lighting schedules can help create the ideal conditions for shrimp spawning and post-larvae growth. Biosecurity measures in the hatchery cannot be overstated, as shrimp are highly susceptible to diseases and pests. Effective biosecurity practices include sterilization of equipment, implementation of quarantine procedures for new broodstock, and regular health monitoring to detect early signs of disease or contamination. Ensuring that pathogens are kept out of the system reduces mortality rates and improves overall hatchery performance.

3.1.3 Selecting Broodstock

Selecting the right broodstock is another critical element of a successful hatchery operation. Healthy, disease-free broodstock should be chosen based on specific criteria such as age, size, and genetic lineage. Shrimp with fast growth rates, good feed conversion efficiency, and strong disease resistance should be prioritized, as they will pass these traits on to their offspring. After selecting broodstock, it is important to acclimatize them to hatchery conditions. This process reduces stress and helps the shrimp adjust to new water quality parameters and temperature, which is essential for successful spawning.

3.1.4 Spawning Techniques

Spawning techniques vary depending on the species of shrimp and the farming method. Induced spawning can be achieved through hormonal treatments or by manipulating environmental factors such as temperature, salinity, and photoperiod. This technique helps synchronize spawning and ensures a consistent supply of larvae. In contrast, natural spawning occurs when the right environmental conditions are provided for shrimp to reproduce without intervention. For successful natural spawning, the hatchery environment must replicate the shrimp's natural habitat, with the right water temperature, salinity, and light cycles to encourage reproduction.

3.2 Larval Rearing Techniques

Larval rearing is a critical phase in shrimp farming, requiring careful attention to ensure the successful development of shrimp larvae from the nauplius stage to post-larvae (PL). Understanding the various larval stages, providing the right nutrition, maintaining optimal water quality, and managing stocking density are all essential components for producing healthy and robust shrimp that can thrive in grow-out systems.

3.2.1 Larval Stages and Development

The development of shrimp larvae occurs in several distinct stages. The larval cycle begins with the nauplius stage, where shrimp larvae are relatively undeveloped and rely on their yolk sac for nutrients. This stage typically lasts 1-2 days. Afterward, larvae enter the zoea stage, during which they begin to feed externally. At this point, they develop swimming appendages and exhibit increased mobility. The zoea stage can last 4-5 days, during which larvae require a well-balanced diet rich in essential nutrients to fuel their rapid growth. The final larval stage is the mysis stage, lasting 3-4 days. During this stage, the larvae develop further into more shrimp-like forms, preparing for the post-larval (PL) stage, where they resemble miniature adult shrimp. The entire larval development process, from nauplius to post-larvae, generally takes about 10-15 days, depending on environmental conditions.

3.2.2 Feeding Practices

Feeding practices are a central aspect of larval rearing. Larvae have specific nutritional requirements that vary across the different developmental stages. In the early nauplius stage, larvae do not require external feeding as they rely on their yolk sac. However, as they transition to the zoea and mysis stages, live feed such as microalgae, rotifers, and Artemia (brine shrimp) become essential to meet their nutritional needs. These feeds provide the necessary proteins, lipids, and essential fatty acids that support the larvae's rapid growth and energy requirements. Protein is especially important during these stages, as it contributes to tissue development, while lipids support energy metabolism. Additionally, it's critical to ensure that larvae receive adequate levels of vitamins and minerals to bolster their immune systems and overall health. Feeding frequency and techniques play a significant role in ensuring that the larvae grow optimally. During the early zoea and mysis stages, shrimp larvae require frequent, small feedings throughout the day. The feeding frequency may range from 4-6 times daily, with feeding intervals evenly spaced to prevent overfeeding and maintain water quality. It's important to monitor feed consumption closely to avoid waste accumulation in the tanks, which could deteriorate water quality. As larvae progress toward the post-larval stage, their feeding habits may shift, allowing for fewer but larger feedings. Shrimp farmers must regularly adjust the quantity and type of feed based on larval growth rates and health, ensuring a nutrient-rich diet without overloading the system.

3.2.3 Water Quality Management for Larvae

Water quality management is another critical factor that directly influences the survival and growth of shrimp larvae. The water environment must be carefully controlled to provide stable conditions that support larval development. Temperature is one of the most important parameters, with the ideal range for most shrimp species being 26-30°C (78-86°F). Maintaining a consistent temperature is crucial, as fluctuations can slow larval development or increase mortality rates. Salinity is another key factor, with optimal salinity levels typically ranging from 28-32 parts per thousand (ppt) for marine shrimp species. pH should be kept within the range of 7.5-8.5 to ensure the larvae thrive, while dissolved oxygen levels should remain above 5-6 mg/L to prevent stress and support respiration. Water exchange systems, whether through regular water changes or recirculating aquaculture systems (RAS), are essential for maintaining these critical water quality parameters. Regular water exchanges help dilute waste, prevent ammonia buildup, and reduce the risk of disease outbreaks, promoting a healthier environment for the larvae.

3.2.4 Stocking Density and Management

Managing stocking density is another important aspect of successful larval rearing. Stocking densities must be carefully calculated to provide enough space for larvae to grow while minimizing competition for resources. In the early stages, stocking densities can be relatively high, but as larvae grow and require more space, densities should be reduced to minimize stress. Higher densities can lead to increased competition for oxygen and food, which can stunt growth and increase the risk of disease. On the other hand, lower densities can improve water quality and encourage faster growth. Striking the right balance is crucial, and regular monitoring of growth rates, behavior, and health indicators will help in making necessary adjustments.

Monitoring the growth and health of shrimp larvae is a key practice during the rearing phase. Farmers should regularly inspect the larvae for signs of stress, disease, or deformities, which can indicate poor water quality or nutritional deficiencies. Monitoring growth rates helps to assess whether the feeding schedule and water conditions are optimal. Corrective actions, such as adjusting feeding practices or enhancing aeration, should be implemented as soon as any issues are detected.

3.2.5 Harvesting Post-Larvae

Harvesting post-larvae is the final step in the larval rearing process, and timing is crucial to ensure the post-larvae are healthy and ready to be transferred to grow-out systems. Post-larvae are typically harvested when they reach a specific developmental stage, characterized by increased size and shrimp-like appearance. Signs of readiness include a shift in coloration and more active swimming behavior. Harvesting should be carried out gently to minimize stress and avoid injury to the shrimp. Post-harvest handling is just as important as the rearing process. Post-larvae must be acclimatized to the new water conditions of the grow-out systems, which often involves gradually adjusting salinity, temperature, and pH to avoid shock. By using drip acclimation or other slow transition techniques, the post-larvae can be safely introduced to their new environment.

3.3 Common Hatchery Challenges and Solutions

Hatcheries are critical in shrimp farming, but they also come with numerous challenges. Disease management, water quality issues, nutritional deficiencies, and environmental stressors are some of the common hurdles farmers face. Identifying and solving these problems is essential for maintaining a healthy and productive shrimp hatchery. Effective record-keeping and data monitoring further help in overcoming these challenges, enabling farmers to optimize their hatchery operations.

3.3.1 Identifying Common Diseases

One of the most significant challenges in shrimp hatcheries is disease management. Shrimp larvae are susceptible to a variety of diseases, many of which can cause devastating losses if not properly addressed. **Viral infections**, such as **White Spot Syndrome Virus (WSSV),** are common and highly contagious, affecting shrimp at all stages of life. WSSV can cause lethargy, loss of appetite, and characteristic white spots on the exoskeleton, often leading to high mortality rates. **Bacterial infections**, such as **Vibrio**, can also pose serious threats, often resulting in **necrosis, shell discoloration, and weakened**

immune responses. **Fungal infections** are less common but can still occur, typically manifesting as fungal growth on the larvae's body, which hampers their movement and feeding. Identifying these diseases early is crucial. Farmers should be vigilant for signs of illness, such as abnormal swimming patterns, loss of appetite, and visible lesions.

Prevention is the best strategy against disease outbreaks in shrimp hatcheries. Biosecurity measures, such as sterilizing equipment, implementing quarantine procedures for new broodstock, and sourcing disease-free shrimp, are essential practices for disease prevention. Water management also plays a critical role in minimizing the risk of infections. Ensuring proper water filtration and regular water exchanges reduces the likelihood of pathogens proliferating in the system. Regular health checks and monitoring larvae for signs of disease can help catch potential outbreaks before they spread. If disease does occur, early treatment is key to minimizing losses. Antibiotics can be used to treat bacterial infections, but their use should be carefully managed to prevent the development of antibiotic-resistant strains. Antiviral treatments for viral infections like WSSV are still under development, but supportive care, such as improving water quality and providing nutrient-rich feed, can help boost the shrimp's immune system. It's important to consult with aquatic veterinarians to develop appropriate treatment plans.

3.3.2 Common Problems

Water quality issues are another common challenge in shrimp hatcheries. Even slight fluctuations in water quality can have significant impacts on the health and growth of shrimp larvae. Common water quality problems include ammonia spikes, which are toxic to shrimp and can result from uneaten feed and waste accumulation. Low dissolved oxygen is another issue, often caused by overcrowding or insufficient aeration. This can lead to hypoxia, causing stress and, eventually, mortality in shrimp larvae. Variations in salinity and pH can also negatively affect larvae, particularly if they occur suddenly, as shrimp are sensitive to changes in their environment. To prevent water quality issues, hatchery managers need to implement effective filtration and aeration systems. Regular water testing should be conducted to monitor key parameters such as ammonia levels, pH, salinity, and dissolved oxygen. Installing biological filtration systems can help control ammonia levels by promoting the growth of beneficial bacteria that break down toxic compounds. In addition, water exchange or recirculating systems should be in place to maintain optimal water conditions. Maintaining stable salinity and pH is crucial for the larvae's overall health, so farmers should monitor these parameters closely, especially during feeding times and after water changes.

3.3.3 Nutritional Deficiencies

Nutritional deficiencies are another challenge that can hinder the growth and survival of shrimp larvae. Poor nutrition can lead to a host of issues, including stunted growth, deformities, and increased susceptibility to diseases. Nutritional problems often arise when larvae do not receive the right balance of proteins, lipids, and essential micronutrients. Shrimp larvae, especially in the zoea and mysis stages, require a diet rich in proteins and essential fatty acids to fuel their rapid growth and energy demands. Deficiencies in these nutrients can result in weak larvae that fail to reach the post-larval stage.

Farmers can identify nutritional deficiencies by observing the growth rates and physical condition of the larvae. Slow growth, deformities such as bent spines, and higher-than-normal mortality rates can all indicate that the shrimp are not receiving the necessary nutrients. To address these issues, it's essential to provide a well-balanced diet that meets the larvae's nutritional needs. Live feeds, such as microalgae and Artemia, should be used alongside formulated feeds to ensure that larvae receive a diverse and nutrient-dense diet. Farmers may also consider supplementing their feed with vitamins, minerals, and essential fatty acids to prevent deficiencies. Adjusting feeding practices, such as increasing feeding frequency or using higher-quality feeds, can further enhance larval health and growth.

3.3.4 Environmental Stressors

Environmental stressors are another factor that can impact the success of a shrimp hatchery. Temperature fluctuations, poor water quality, and overcrowding are all common stressors that can negatively affect shrimp larvae. Stress can weaken the immune system, making the larvae more susceptible to diseases and reducing their overall survival rates. For example, sudden changes in temperature can cause larvae to become lethargic or stressed, slowing down their development and increasing their vulnerability to disease. Mitigating environmental stressors requires careful management of the hatchery environment. Temperature should be closely monitored and maintained within the optimal range for the shrimp species being farmed. Using heaters, chillers, and insulation can help stabilize water temperature, reducing the likelihood of harmful fluctuations. Maintaining appropriate stocking densities is also crucial, as overcrowded tanks can lead to competition for food and oxygen, increasing stress levels among the larvae. Feeding practices should be optimized to ensure that all larvae receive sufficient food without overfeeding, which can degrade water quality and cause additional stress.

3.3.5 Record Keeping and Monitoring

Record-keeping and monitoring are essential tools for managing a shrimp hatchery successfully. Maintaining detailed records of water quality parameters, feeding schedules, health assessments, and growth rates allows farmers to identify patterns and potential problems early. For example, if water quality tests consistently show high ammonia levels, adjustments to filtration or feeding practices can be made before it affects the larvae's health. Similarly, tracking growth rates can help identify nutritional deficiencies or other issues that may be hindering the larvae's development. Data collection also provides a valuable resource for continuous improvement in hatchery management. By analyzing trends over time, farmers can adjust their practices to improve the overall efficiency and productivity of their operations.

For instance, data might reveal that certain feeding schedules result in better growth rates, or that specific water management strategies lead to lower disease incidence. Using this data-driven approach, shrimp farmers can make informed decisions that lead to healthier larvae, higher survival rates, and more successful hatchery operations.

CHAPTER 4

FEED AND NUTRITION

4.1 Shrimp Nutritional Needs

Understanding the nutritional needs of shrimp is fundamental to their growth, health, and survival in farming environments. Proper nutrition supports not only their physical development but also their immune system, reproductive capabilities, and resistance to disease. Each stage of a shrimp's life has distinct nutritional requirements, which must be met through a well-balanced diet that includes essential macronutrients and micronutrients. Understanding the digestive physiology of shrimp also helps in formulating and delivering the right types of feed that can be efficiently utilized by shrimp to meet these nutritional demands.

4.1.1 Essential Nutrients

1. **Macronutrients:** Macronutrients—proteins, fats (lipids), and carbohydrates—are the primary building blocks for shrimp health and growth. These are required in relatively large amounts, and their balance in the shrimp's diet determines the shrimp's overall development and productivity.

- **Proteins:** Proteins are perhaps the most critical macronutrient for shrimp, as they are directly involved in building and repairing tissues, including the exoskeleton. Shrimp are known to have high protein requirements, especially during the early growth phases and molting periods, where protein is vital for the formation of new body tissue and the shedding of the old exoskeleton. High-protein feed typically contains fishmeal, plant proteins, or specially formulated commercial protein supplements, which support rapid growth and improve survival rates.

- **Fats (Lipids):** Fats provide a concentrated source of energy, essential for shrimp metabolism and energy-intensive processes like molting and reproduction. Lipids, particularly essential fatty acids like omega-3 and omega-6, are necessary for the development of cell membranes, hormone production, and maintaining healthy immune function. Marine-based oils or microalgae are often incorporated into feeds to provide these necessary lipids.
- **Carbohydrates:** Carbohydrates serve as an energy source but are less crucial for shrimp compared to proteins and lipids. While carbohydrates are important for energy metabolism, shrimp have a limited ability to digest

certain complex carbohydrates. Simple sugars and starches are often included in shrimp feed to support energy needs, but they must be carefully balanced to avoid compromising water quality and creating digestive issues.

2. **Micronutrients:** Micronutrients, though required in smaller quantities than macronutrients, are equally vital to the overall health of shrimp. These include vitamins and minerals, which support a range of metabolic and physiological functions.

- **Vitamins:** Shrimp require a variety of vitamins for growth, immune function, and maintaining normal physiological processes. For example:
  - ✓ Vitamin A is essential for growth and vision development in shrimp.

- ✓ Vitamin D is involved in calcium and phosphorus regulation, which is important for shell formation.
- ✓ Vitamin E acts as an antioxidant, protecting shrimp from cellular damage and improving stress resistance.
- ✓ B-complex vitamins support energy metabolism and nervous system function, helping shrimp utilize nutrients more efficiently.
- **Minerals:** Minerals play key roles in shrimp metabolism and overall health. Calcium and phosphorus are essential for exoskeleton formation and repair, especially during molting. Trace elements like zinc, copper, and manganese are also crucial for enzymatic functions, immune system health, and reproductive success. Because shrimp live in water, they absorb some minerals

directly from their environment, but supplementation through feed is often necessary to ensure adequate intake, particularly in intensive farming systems.

4.1.2 Growth Stages and Nutritional Requirements

- **Nauplius Stage:** The nauplius stage is the earliest stage of shrimp larval development, where their nutritional needs are highly specialized. Nauplii rely primarily on live feed such as rotifers and microalgae, which provide essential nutrients, particularly proteins and fatty acids necessary for early growth and survival. During this stage, nauplii have limited digestive capabilities, so providing feed that is easily digestible and nutrient-rich is crucial. Microalgae like Chaetoceros and Tetraselmis are commonly used because they are not only easy for nauplii to digest but are also excellent sources of essential fatty acids that aid in the early development of organs and the exoskeleton.

- **Post-Larval Stage:** As shrimp progress into the post-larval stage, their nutritional needs become more complex, and they can start to consume more diverse and complex feeds. The diet during this stage shifts from primarily live feed to more formulated feed that can include a combination of microalgae, zooplankton, and commercial pellets. Protein remains a key component, as shrimp in this stage experience rapid growth and require substantial energy to support this development. The introduction of high-protein feeds rich in essential amino acids and fatty acids, alongside live feeds, ensures that post-larvae have the nutrients necessary for robust development and a healthy immune system.

- **Juvenile and Adult Stages:** Once shrimp reach the juvenile and adult stages, their nutritional requirements are geared toward supporting continued growth, reproduction, and molting. Juveniles need a nutrient-dense diet to maintain fast growth rates, while adults also require feeds that support reproductive health and maintain the quality of their exoskeleton. Protein-rich diets remain critical, but the balance of fats and carbohydrates becomes more important, especially for energy demands. Lipids, particularly essential fatty acids, support reproduction, while minerals like calcium and phosphorus are needed in larger amounts to support continuous molting and shell hardening. Commercial feeds for adults are often carefully balanced to meet these needs and can include prebiotics and probiotics to support digestive health.

4.1.3 Digestive Physiology of Shrimp

The digestive system of shrimp is relatively simple but specialized, consisting of three main parts: the foregut, midgut, and hindgut. Each of these sections plays a critical role in how shrimp process and absorb nutrients, and understanding this system is key to providing the right types of feed.

- **Foregut:** The foregut, also known as the stomach, is where the initial breakdown of food occurs. The foregut contains gastric teeth that grind the food into smaller particles, allowing digestive enzymes to work more efficiently. This mechanical breakdown is crucial since shrimp consume a variety of feed types, ranging from live organisms to formulated pellets.

- **Midgut:** The midgut is the primary site for digestion and nutrient absorption. It contains the hepatopancreas, a multifunctional organ that produces digestive enzymes and helps in the absorption of digested nutrients. The hepatopancreas plays a vital role in processing proteins, fats, and carbohydrates, making it a key component in the shrimp's digestive efficiency. Any feed that shrimp consume must be formulated to ensure it can be efficiently broken down by the enzymes produced in the midgut, particularly for macronutrients like proteins and fats.

- **Hindgut:** The hindgut is responsible for expelling undigested waste material. Although it does not play a major role in digestion, maintaining the health of the hindgut is important for overall digestive health, as poor water quality or imbalanced diets can lead to gut disorders and impact feed conversion efficiency.

4.2 Commercial Feeds Vs Natural Feeds

Understanding the differences between commercial and natural feeds is essential for optimizing shrimp nutrition and growth. Each type of feed has its own advantages and limitations, and knowing how to integrate them effectively can help shrimp farmers achieve balanced nutrition, improve growth rates, and maintain overall shrimp health. In shrimp farming, the choice between commercial feeds and natural feeds often depends on the specific needs of the shrimp at different life stages, environmental conditions, and farm management goals.

4.2.1 Types of Commercial Feeds

- **Pelleted Feeds:** Pelleted feeds are the most commonly used type of commercial feed in shrimp farming. They come in various forms, such as pellets, crumbles, and powders, to suit different stages of shrimp growth. Pelleted feeds are engineered to be nutrient-dense, ensuring that the shrimp receive a balanced intake of proteins, fats, carbohydrates, vitamins, and minerals.

- ✓ **Pellets:** Typically used for larger shrimp (juvenile and adult stages), pellets are designed to float or sink slowly, making them easily accessible to shrimp. The size of the pellets is chosen based on the shrimp's size and feeding habits. Pellets can also be produced in slow-sinking or fast-sinking varieties, depending on the feeding behavior of the shrimp species.

- ✓ **Crumbles and Powders:** Crumbles and powders are finer feeds suitable for shrimp in their early post-larval stages. These feed forms ensure that even small larvae can consume the particles easily and receive the necessary nutrients during their rapid growth phases.

The convenience of pelleted feeds lies in their consistent size, shape, and nutrient content, allowing for precise feeding and minimizing waste in the pond or tank environment.

- **Formulated Feeds:** Formulated feeds are specially designed to meet the exact nutritional needs of shrimp at different life stages, from larvae to adult. These feeds are typically manufactured using high-quality ingredients such as fishmeal, soybean meal, wheat flour, and other marine or plant-based proteins, as well as added lipids and essential fatty acids. The goal is to create a balanced diet that provides the right amounts of macronutrients (proteins, fats, and carbohydrates) and micronutrients (vitamins and minerals) required for optimal shrimp health. Formulated feeds are often fortified with:
  - ✓ Essential amino acids that are crucial for growth.

- ✓ Fatty acids like omega-3 and omega-6, which support healthy immune function and reproductive health.
- ✓ Vitamins (such as A, D, E, and B-complex) and minerals (like calcium and phosphorus) to promote proper metabolic function and exoskeleton development.

These feeds are tested for consistency and quality, which helps farmers achieve predictable growth outcomes in shrimp farming operations.

4.2.2 Benefits and Drawbacks
Commercial Feeds

- **Benefits:**
  - **Nutritional Consistency:** Commercial feeds are formulated to provide a balanced, controlled nutrient profile that meets the specific dietary requirements of shrimp at each stage of growth. This eliminates the guesswork

and ensures that the shrimp receive the right nutrients consistently.

- **Convenience:** Commercial feeds are easy to store, handle, and distribute, saving farmers time and effort. The ability to precisely measure and distribute feed helps with feed management, reducing wastage and ensuring that shrimp receive the correct rations.

- **Optimized Growth:** With a precise balance of proteins, fats, and essential nutrients, commercial feeds are designed to promote optimal growth and development, improving feed conversion ratios (FCR) and reducing the time to harvest.

- **Drawbacks:**

✓ **Cost:** Commercial feeds can be expensive, especially if they are premium or high-quality feeds. The cost factor can increase the overall production expenses for shrimp farmers, particularly in large-scale operations.

- ✓ **Dependency on a Single Source of Nutrition:** Sole reliance on commercial feeds can limit the natural diversity of the shrimp's diet. Although these feeds are nutritionally balanced, they may not fully mimic the variety of nutrients and feeding behaviors that shrimp would experience in the wild.

- ✓ **Environmental Impact:** Some commercial feeds, especially those high in fishmeal, contribute to overfishing or unsustainable practices in sourcing ingredients. Additionally, uneaten pellets can contribute to water pollution if not managed properly.

4.2.3 Natural Feeds
- **Benefits:**
  - ✓ **Mimicking Natural Feeding Behaviors:** Natural feeds like live organisms (copepods,

Artemia, rotifers) or organic materials (vegetable matter, detritus) promote natural foraging behaviors in shrimp. This enhances their overall health and improves their gut flora, contributing to better digestion and immune system strength.

- ✓ **Improved Gut Health:** Natural feeds often contain microorganisms and bioactive compounds that support the shrimp's digestive system. The inclusion of live or natural feed can promote the development of beneficial gut bacteria, leading to better nutrient absorption and overall health.
- ✓ **Cost-Effective:** In some cases, natural feeds, particularly those derived from the farm's ecosystem, can be less expensive than commercial alternatives. For example, encouraging the growth of natural plankton in

grow-out ponds or harvesting vegetable matter from local sources can reduce feed costs.

- **Drawbacks:**
  - ✓ **Inconsistent Nutrient Profile:** Natural feeds can vary widely in nutrient content, making it difficult to ensure that shrimp are receiving all the necessary nutrients in the right proportions. This inconsistency can lead to nutritional deficiencies or imbalances if not carefully managed.
  - ✓ **Labor Intensive:** Rearing or harvesting natural feeds like live copepods or Artemia can be time-consuming and require additional space and resources. Managing live feeds also demands precise control over water quality, aeration, and feeding systems.
  - ✓ **Limited Availability:** Depending on the farm's location and environmental conditions,

natural feeds may not always be available in sufficient quantities to meet the shrimp's needs. This could require supplementation with commercial feeds to ensure consistent growth.

4.2.4 Feeding Strategies

- **Combined Feeding Approaches:** One of the most effective strategies in shrimp farming is combining commercial feeds with natural feeds to enhance both nutrition and shrimp well-being. This integrated feeding approach takes advantage of the balanced nutrition offered by commercial feeds while also benefiting from the variety and natural foraging behaviors provided by natural feeds.
  - ✓ **Enhanced Nutrition:** By providing a mixed diet that includes both commercial and natural feeds, shrimp receive a more diverse nutrient profile, including essential amino acids, fatty

acids, and bioactive compounds that may not be present in commercial feeds alone.

- ✓ **Promoting Growth and Survival:** Studies have shown that shrimp fed a combination of commercial and natural feeds often exhibit better growth rates, improved survival, and enhanced stress resistance, compared to shrimp fed only one type of feed.
- ✓ **Natural Behavior Stimulation:** The inclusion of natural feeds encourages shrimp to engage in foraging behaviors, which reduces stress and improves their overall health. This can lead to better feed utilization and improved shrimp welfare.

- **Considerations for Feed Selection:** When choosing between commercial and natural feeds, or a combination of both, several factors should be taken into consideration:

- ✓ **Life Stage:** The nutritional needs of shrimp change as they grow, so selecting the appropriate feed for each stage—from nauplii to post-larvae to adult—is critical. Larvae, for example, benefit greatly from live feed like microalgae and rotifers, while juveniles and adults can thrive on a mix of commercial and natural feeds.
- ✓ **Growth Rate:** High-growth phases, particularly during molting or reproductive periods, require protein-rich diets with additional essential nutrients to support tissue regeneration and reproductive health.
- ✓ **Water Quality:** Uneaten feed, especially commercial pellets, can impact water quality by contributing to ammonia and nitrate buildup. It's important to manage feeding carefully to avoid overfeeding and maintain water quality.

- ✓ **Specific Nutritional Needs:** Different shrimp species may have unique nutritional requirements that affect feed choices. For example, marine shrimp species may require higher levels of certain fatty acids, while freshwater species might benefit from different protein sources or feed textures.

4.3 Feeding Schedules and Best Practices

4.3.1 Establishing Feeding Schedules

Establishing feeding schedules for shrimp is a critical aspect of shrimp farming, as it directly influences growth rates, feed efficiency, and overall health. Feeding frequencies should be carefully tailored to the shrimp's life stages. For younger shrimp, such as larvae and post-larvae, more frequent feedings are essential due to their rapid growth and higher metabolic rates. At this stage, feeding several times a day ensures that they receive a consistent supply of nutrients, promoting healthy development and reducing stress. As shrimp mature into juveniles and adults, the feeding frequency can be reduced, but it is still important to maintain a regular schedule to support steady growth. Regular feeding minimizes periods of hunger, which can stress shrimp and slow growth. Determining the correct amount of feed is equally important. Feed amounts should be calculated based on the shrimp's biomass, their growth rates, and the environmental conditions in the farming system, particularly water quality. Overfeeding can lead to wasted feed, which in turn can pollute the water and cause spikes in ammonia and other harmful substances. Underfeeding, on the other hand, can slow shrimp growth and weaken their immune systems. To ensure optimal feeding, shrimp farmers should closely monitor feed consumption and adjust feeding rates accordingly. One common approach is to use feeding trays or systems that allow the farmer to observe the amount of uneaten feed and make necessary adjustments.

4.3.2 Feeding Methods

Various feeding techniques are used in shrimp farming, and the choice of method depends on the specific setup and shrimp population. Broadcast feeding, where feed is scattered across the water surface, is commonly used in larger ponds or tanks and allows shrimp to forage naturally. However, it can sometimes result in uneven feed distribution, especially in areas with strong water currents. Targeted feeding, where feed is distributed more precisely to specific areas, can be more efficient, especially in high-density environments. Automatic feeders are also popular in commercial operations because they allow for more controlled and consistent feeding schedules. These devices can be programmed to release precise amounts of feed at specific times, improving feed efficiency and reducing waste.

Monitoring feed quality is crucial for maintaining shrimp health. High-quality feeds should be used to ensure that shrimp receive the necessary nutrients for growth and immune function. Feed spoilage or contamination can introduce pathogens into the system and negatively impact shrimp health. Farmers should store feed in cool, dry conditions to prevent mold, spoilage, or nutrient degradation. Checking the feed for freshness and nutrient content before use is a best practice that helps maintain the overall health of the shrimp.

4.3.3 Behavioral Observations

Behavioral observations during feeding are an important tool for shrimp farmers. Shrimp feeding behavior can provide insight into their health and the effectiveness of the feeding program. Healthy shrimp will typically show an active and aggressive feeding response, gathering near feeding areas and consuming the feed quickly. If shrimp appear sluggish, disinterested in feed, or if significant amounts of feed are left uneaten, this could indicate underlying health issues, poor water quality, or that the feed amounts need adjustment. Continuous monitoring of shrimp behavior allows for timely adjustments in feeding practices.

4.3.4 Adjusting Feeding Practices

Environmental factors play a major role in feeding schedules and nutrient requirements. Water temperature, for instance, directly affects shrimp metabolism. In colder water, shrimp tend to eat less and have slower digestion, meaning feeding amounts should be reduced to avoid overfeeding. Conversely, in warmer water, their metabolic rates increase, and they will require more frequent feedings. Similarly, other water parameters such as salinity and dissolved oxygen levels can impact shrimp's appetite and growth rates. Feeding schedules and amounts should be adjusted in response to changes in these environmental factors to optimize shrimp health and feed efficiency. In addition to environmental monitoring, it is critical to continuously assess shrimp health to fine-tune feeding practices. Stress, disease, or signs of poor health, such as abnormal growth rates, discoloration, or increased mortality, may require adjustments to feeding schedules or the introduction of specialized feeds that support immune function or recovery. When health problems arise, farmers should also consider reducing feed amounts to prevent the accumulation of uneaten feed, which can worsen water quality and exacerbate health issues.

4.4 Enhancing Shrimp Growth and Health

4.4.1 Nutritional Supplements

Enhancing shrimp growth and health involves a multifaceted approach that combines nutrition, environmental management, and strategic feeding practices. One key element is the use of nutritional supplements, which play a significant role in optimizing shrimp performance and resilience. Supplements such as probiotics and prebiotics support gut health by fostering beneficial bacteria, which can improve nutrient absorption and digestion. This promotes more efficient feed utilization, leading to better growth rates. Additionally, essential fatty acids, especially omega-3s, are crucial for maintaining cell membrane integrity and supporting immune function, helping shrimp resist diseases and stressors more effectively. The proper formulation and application of these supplements are vital. Timing the introduction of probiotics or fatty acids during critical growth phases can yield significant benefits. Dosage should be tailored to the specific requirements of the shrimp species, considering factors like growth stage, feed composition, and environmental conditions.

4.4.2 Feeding for Stress Reduction

Nutrition also plays a pivotal role in reducing stress among shrimp populations. Environmental stressors—such as fluctuations in water temperature, changes in salinity, or sudden shifts in water quality—can weaken shrimp immune systems, making them more susceptible to diseases. By providing a balanced diet rich in essential nutrients, shrimp farmers can bolster the shrimp's ability to cope with these challenges. High-quality protein and balanced fats help maintain energy levels, while vitamins like vitamin C and E play crucial roles in stress resistance and recovery from environmental fluctuations. Furthermore, managing feeding practices, such as ensuring consistent feeding schedules and avoiding overfeeding, helps mitigate the buildup of waste products that can degrade water quality, reducing a common source of stress. Other stress management strategies include improving water aeration, maintaining stable temperatures, and offering habitat enrichment—like hiding structures or plants—that mimic natural environments, giving shrimp places to retreat and feel secure.

4.4.3 Evaluating Growth Performance

Evaluating growth performance is another essential aspect of enhancing shrimp health. Key metrics such as the feed conversion ratio (FCR), which measures how efficiently shrimp convert feed into body mass, are crucial indicators of growth efficiency. A low FCR suggests that shrimp are utilizing feed well, while a high FCR might indicate wastage or inefficiencies in feed formulation. Survival rates, growth rates, and even shrimp size uniformity across the population are additional indicators of overall farm health. Monitoring these metrics regularly allows farmers to track shrimp development, spot potential problems early, and make necessary adjustments to feeding or farm management. For instance, if growth rates are lagging behind expectations, it could point to a nutritional deficiency, prompting the introduction of more nutrient-dense feed or supplements. Shrimp farmers can also use growth data to refine and adjust their nutritional strategies. Feed formulations should be optimized based on performance data to provide the necessary nutrients at each growth stage. For instance, during early post-larval stages, a high-protein diet may be critical for rapid growth, but as shrimp mature, the focus could shift towards maintaining energy levels and supporting reproductive health. Adjusting feed composition in response to real-time growth performance ensures that shrimp are receiving the optimal balance of nutrients for their specific life stage.

4.4.4 Research and Innovation in Shrimp Nutrition
Research and innovation in shrimp nutrition are constantly evolving, driven by the need to improve feed efficiency, reduce costs, and support sustainable

practices. One emerging trend is the exploration of alternative protein sources for shrimp diets. Traditional fishmeal, a primary ingredient in shrimp feed, is becoming more expensive and less sustainable. Researchers are investigating options like insect meal, derived from sources like black soldier fly larvae, and plant-based proteins like soy or algae. These alternatives can potentially reduce the environmental impact of shrimp farming while maintaining, or even improving, growth performance. Innovations in feed formulation are also focusing on enhancing the digestibility and nutritional value of plant-based ingredients, ensuring they can serve as viable replacements for animal-derived proteins. Looking to the future, continued research and development in shrimp nutrition and feed technology hold the potential to revolutionize shrimp farming. Advancements in precision feeding technology, for instance, are enabling farmers to deliver feed more accurately and efficiently, minimizing waste and improving FCR. Additionally, ongoing research into the use of bioactive compounds—such as immunostimulants and growth enhancers—could lead to more resilient shrimp populations that require fewer antibiotics or chemical treatments. As the shrimp farming industry continues to grow, the integration of these new approaches will be essential for meeting the demands of sustainability, productivity, and profitability. The future of shrimp nutrition will likely see more personalized feed strategies tailored to specific environmental conditions and genetic strains, further optimizing shrimp health and farm performance

CHAPTER 5

SHRIMP HEALTH MANAGEMENT

5.1 Recognizing Common Shrimp Diseases

Recognizing common shrimp diseases is critical for maintaining healthy shrimp populations and minimizing potential economic losses. Shrimp diseases can be broadly classified into viral, bacterial, fungal, and parasitic categories, each with its unique symptoms, causes, and consequences. Early detection and timely intervention are key to reducing disease outbreaks, as diseases can spread rapidly in densely populated aquaculture environments.

5.1.1 Viral Diseases

Viral diseases pose a significant threat to shrimp farms due to their ability to spread quickly and cause severe mortality. One of the most notorious viral infections is **White Spot Syndrome Virus (WSSV).** Shrimp infected with WSSV exhibit classic symptoms like white spots on their exoskeleton, lethargy, reduced feed intake, and high mortality rates, often within days of infection. This virus spreads through water, contact with infected shrimp, and contaminated equipment, making biosecurity measures essential in controlling its transmission. Infected farms can suffer massive economic losses if left untreated due to the rapid decline in shrimp populations. Another viral threat is **Taura Syndrome Virus (TSV),** which primarily affects juvenile shrimp. TSV manifests through symptoms such as reddish discoloration of the shrimp's body, soft shells, and rapid death. Poor water quality, stress, and high stocking densities are key factors that increase the risk of TSV outbreaks. Ensuring proper farm management and maintaining optimal environmental conditions can reduce the likelihood of this virus taking hold. **Yellow Head Virus (YHV)** is another viral infection that shrimp farmers must monitor. Infected shrimp develop pale yellowing of the head and body, exhibit erratic swimming behavior, and often experience sudden death. YHV spreads quickly in shrimp farms, and early detection through diagnostic tools such as PCR (Polymerase Chain Reaction) tests can be crucial for containing the outbreak before it devastates the population. Regular monitoring and screening for viruses are essential in keeping YHV and other viral infections under control.

5.1.2 Bacterial Diseases

Bacterial diseases are also prevalent in shrimp farming, with vibriosis being one of the most common. **Vibrio species** can infect shrimp through wounds or compromised exoskeletons, leading to symptoms such as shell lesions, red or pink discoloration, sluggish behavior, and slow growth. Vibriosis is often triggered by poor water quality, high levels of organic matter, and stress within the shrimp population. Maintaining good water quality and reducing organic buildup are critical steps in preventing the spread of this bacterial infection. Another severe bacterial infection is **Necrotizing Hepatopancreatitis (NHP),** which affects the hepatopancreas, an organ essential for shrimp digestion and metabolism. Shrimp suffering from NHP display pale bodies, reduced feed intake, and sluggish behavior. The damage to the hepatopancreas severely hampers the shrimp's ability to process nutrients, leading to stunted growth and increased mortality. High temperatures, poor water quality, and stress are known risk factors for NHP, making environmental management crucial in preventing outbreaks.

5.1.3 Fungal Diseases

Fungal diseases, although less common than viral or bacterial infections, can still cause significant damage, especially in farms with poor water circulation and high organic loads. **Fusarium infections** are characterized by cotton-like growths on the shrimp's body and legs. These infections can spread quickly in stagnant water environments, where organic matter accumulates. Improving water circulation, reducing organic loads, and regular cleaning of shrimp farming equipment can help prevent these fungal outbreaks. **Lagenidium** is another fungal disease that affects shrimp, causing soft tissue necrosis and leg deformities. This infection thrives in unsanitary conditions where dead shrimp are not promptly removed, and water quality is compromised. By maintaining clean farm conditions and ensuring that dead or diseased shrimp are swiftly removed, the spread of Lagenidium can be mitigated.

5.1.4 Parasitic Diseases

Parasitic diseases also pose a significant threat to shrimp farming operations, with **Enterocytozoon hepatopenaei (EHP)** being one of the most damaging parasitic infections. EHP is a microsporidian parasite that targets the *hepatopancreas,* similar to NHP, leading to slow growth, poor feed conversion, and significant production losses. EHP is primarily transmitted through contaminated water and feed, making proper farm hygiene and the use of disease-free feed essential to prevent outbreaks. Once EHP takes hold, it can be challenging to eradicate from the farm, underscoring the importance of preventive measures.

The successful management of shrimp diseases requires not only recognizing symptoms early but also implementing robust biosecurity measures, maintaining optimal water quality, and ensuring proper nutrition. Regular monitoring, using diagnostic tools like PCR tests, and adhering to strict farm hygiene practices can help prevent the spread of diseases. By taking proactive steps, shrimp farmers can protect their shrimp populations and sustain the long-term health and productivity of their farms.

5.2 Preventative Measures and Health Monitoring

Preventative measures and health monitoring are essential pillars in maintaining a thriving shrimp farm. The old adage "prevention is better than cure" applies strongly to shrimp farming, where the emphasis on keeping shrimp healthy and minimizing the risk of disease outbreaks can save both time and resources. Effective prevention strategies hinge on biosecurity protocols, farm hygiene, continuous health monitoring, and optimized nutrition for shrimp immunity.

5.2.1 Biosecurity Protocols

One of the most crucial aspects of disease prevention in shrimp farming is the establishment of strict biosecurity protocols. **Quarantine practices** should be a top priority, especially when introducing new shrimp or broodstock into the farm. By isolating these shrimp in quarantine facilities for a period of 2-4 weeks, farmers can ensure that any potential diseases or pathogens present in the new stock do not spread to the existing shrimp population. During this quarantine phase, farmers should closely monitor the shrimp for any signs of illness, such as unusual behavior, lesions, or discoloration, and treat any health issues before introducing the shrimp into the main farming area. **Equipment disinfection** is another key component of biosecurity. Farming equipment such as nets, feeders, and water pumps can act as vectors for disease transmission if not properly cleaned. Regular disinfection using chemicals like chlorine or iodine can help eliminate potential pathogens on tools and equipment, ensuring a sanitized environment for the shrimp. It's also important to clean equipment after each use and between farming cycles, reducing the risk of cross-contamination. **Water quality management** plays a critical role in preventing shrimp diseases, as poor water conditions can lead to stress, weakened immune systems, and increased susceptibility to pathogens. Farmers should maintain optimal levels of pH, salinity, temperature, and dissolved oxygen in shrimp ponds or tanks, as fluctuations in these parameters can create an environment conducive to disease outbreaks. The regular use of water testing kits allows farmers to monitor these water quality parameters closely, enabling early detection of imbalances that could harm shrimp health. Routine screening and testing of shrimp are vital preventative practices. Regular health screenings, such as PCR (Polymerase Chain Reaction) tests and microscopic examinations, can detect the presence of viral, bacterial, or parasitic infections before they spread. Early detection through testing provides an opportunity for farmers to take immediate action and contain potential disease outbreaks, safeguarding the health of the entire shrimp population.

5.2.2 Farm Hygiene and Sanitation

Farm hygiene and sanitation also play a significant role in disease prevention. Cleaning protocols should be established and followed strictly, especially between farming cycles. Ponds or tanks need to be cleaned thoroughly to remove biofilm, organic matter, and any lingering disease-causing pathogens. This includes draining the water, scrubbing surfaces, and using disinfectants to eliminate contaminants. Regular waste management practices, such as removing uneaten feed and dead shrimp, are equally important in preventing the buildup of harmful organic loads that can attract pathogens. Continuous monitoring of shrimp health is crucial for early detection of potential health issues. Behavioral observations are an excellent first line of defense. Farmers should pay close attention to daily feeding patterns, swimming activity, and overall behavior of their shrimp. Changes such as reduced feeding, erratic swimming, or altered coloration can signal underlying stress or illness, prompting further investigation. In addition to behavioral monitoring, physical examinations of shrimp should be conducted regularly. Checking for signs of disease such as lesions, discoloration, deformities, or soft shells can help catch infections early. Regular physical health checks allow farmers to intervene promptly with treatments, reducing the chance of disease spreading throughout the shrimp population. Record keeping is another often overlooked, yet vital, component of shrimp health monitoring. Maintaining detailed records on water quality parameters, growth rates, health checks, and feed consumption helps farmers track the overall performance of their shrimp. This data can be analyzed to identify trends, enabling farmers to detect early warning signs of potential health issues or environmental imbalances. For example, if growth rates start to decline, the records may reveal changes in water quality or feed efficiency that need to be addressed.

5.2.3 Nutrition and Immunity

Nutrition is fundamental to shrimp immunity and overall health. Providing a well-balanced, high-quality feed that meets the shrimp's nutritional needs ensures they develop strong immune systems, making them more resilient to diseases. Nutrition not only fuels growth but also supports essential biological functions that help shrimp resist infections. In this regard, using high-quality, nutrient-rich feeds is an effective strategy for bolstering shrimp immune health. Probiotics and prebiotics have emerged as valuable nutritional supplements that can significantly enhance shrimp gut health and overall immunity. Probiotics introduce beneficial bacteria into the shrimp's digestive system, helping to maintain a healthy balance of gut flora. This supports the shrimp's ability to digest feed efficiently while also boosting immune function. Prebiotics, on the other hand, act as food for these beneficial bacteria, encouraging their growth and activity. By incorporating probiotics and prebiotics into shrimp feed, farmers can not only improve feed conversion rates but also reduce the incidence of gut-related diseases, contributing to overall farm health.

5.3 Treatment Methods and Biosecurity Protocols

In shrimp farming, managing disease outbreaks effectively requires a combination of treatment methods and robust biosecurity protocols. Understanding and implementing the right strategies can mitigate the impact of disease, safeguard shrimp populations, and protect the long-term sustainability of the farm.

5.3.1 Disease Treatment Approaches

One of the primary approaches to treating shrimp diseases is the use of **antibiotics**. However, responsible use of antibiotics is essential to avoid contributing to the growing problem of antibiotic resistance. Farmers should only administer antibiotics when absolutely necessary and under the guidance of a qualified veterinarian. Antibiotic treatments should be targeted and specific, and broad-spectrum antibiotics should be avoided unless recommended by a veterinary professional. Common antibiotics used in shrimp farming include **oxytetracycline** and **florfenicol.** These antibiotics are typically administered via medicated feeds or directly into the water, depending on the disease being treated. Correct application and dosage are critical to ensure the antibiotics are effective while minimizing the risk of resistance. Farmers should follow veterinary prescriptions closely, and all antibiotic treatments should be documented. Adhering to withdrawal periods after antibiotic use is also crucial. The withdrawal period is the time required between the last antibiotic treatment and the harvesting of shrimp.

During this period, the antibiotic residues are eliminated from the shrimp's system. This step ensures that no harmful antibiotic residues remain in the shrimp when they are sold or consumed, which is important for food safety and regulatory compliance.

5.3.2 Probiotic Treatments

As an alternative to antibiotics, many shrimp farmers are turning to probiotics. Probiotics are eco-friendly treatments that help promote the growth of beneficial bacteria in the shrimp's gut, improving digestion and boosting immune responses. By strengthening the shrimp's natural defenses, probiotics help reduce the need for antibiotics and can be used preventatively to avoid bacterial infections. Probiotics can be applied in different ways, such as mixing them into the shrimp's feed or introducing them into the water in ponds or tanks. When used in water, probiotics not only benefit the shrimp but also help improve water quality by breaking down organic matter and reducing harmful bacteria.

5.3.3 Vaccines and Immunostimulants

Vaccines and immunostimulants represent another promising area in disease prevention and treatment in shrimp farming. While still in the early stages of development, vaccines could provide shrimp with immunity to certain viral and bacterial diseases, reducing the risk of outbreaks. Immunostimulants, which enhance the shrimp's natural immune response, are already being explored as a way to help shrimp resist infections. These technologies offer hope for reducing dependence on antibiotics and other chemical treatments, but there are still challenges to overcome, such as developing effective delivery methods and ensuring broad coverage against different pathogens.

5.3.4 Isolation and Containment

In the event of a disease outbreak, biosecurity protocols become critically important. One of the first steps is to implement **strict isolation and containment measures**. Infected ponds or tanks should be quarantined immediately to prevent the spread of the disease to other areas of the farm. This may involve stopping the movement of equipment, people, and water between affected and unaffected areas. **Disinfection and sterilization** are essential after a disease outbreak. Ponds or tanks should be drained completely, and all surfaces, including the substrate, should be thoroughly cleaned and disinfected. Chlorine or iodine-based disinfectants are commonly used to eliminate pathogens. Once the cleaning process is complete, the ponds or tanks should be allowed to dry fully before restocking with healthy shrimp. This break period helps reduce the risk of reintroducing pathogens. In severe cases, culling of infected shrimp populations may be necessary, particularly with highly contagious diseases like White Spot Syndrome Virus (WSSV) or Yellow Head Virus (YHV). While this step is difficult, it is sometimes the only way to prevent the disease from spreading further. Culling should be done humanely and followed by thorough disinfection of the area.

Improving farm management practices is another critical aspect of preventing disease outbreaks. Regular health checks of the shrimp population allow for early detection of disease symptoms, such as changes in behavior, feeding patterns, or physical appearance. Early detection gives farmers a chance to intervene before the disease spreads. Water quality is a key factor in shrimp health, and maintaining optimal water conditions can help prevent diseases. Advanced water recirculation and filtration systems are beneficial for controlling water quality, as they help remove waste, excess feed, and harmful bacteria. These systems can also help regulate parameters like pH, salinity, and dissolved oxygen, reducing stress on the shrimp and making them less susceptible to disease. **Sourcing disease-free broodstock** is another preventative measure that can reduce the introduction of pathogens into a shrimp farm. Broodstock obtained from certified hatcheries that test for common shrimp diseases, such as WSSV or TSV (Taura Syndrome Virus), is less likely to carry infections. By starting with healthy, disease-free shrimp, farmers can significantly lower the risk of disease outbreaks on their farm.

CHAPTER 6

WATER QUALITY AND ENVIRONMENTAL CONTROL

6.1 The Importance of Water Quality for Shrimp Health

Water quality is a critical factor in shrimp farming, influencing shrimp growth, health, disease resistance, and overall productivity. Healthy water conditions are essential for shrimp to thrive, while poor water quality can stress shrimp, reduce survival rates, and lead to costly disease outbreaks. To ensure successful farming operations, shrimp farmers must closely monitor and manage water quality parameters.

6.1.1 Role of Water Quality in Shrimp Physiology

1. **Oxygen Uptake and Metabolism:** Shrimp, like all aquatic animals, rely on dissolved oxygen (DO) in the water for respiration. Shrimp extract oxygen from the water through their gills, and this oxygen is necessary for their metabolic processes,

including growth and energy production. Dissolved oxygen levels should ideally be kept above 5 ppm (parts per million). When oxygen levels drop too low (below 3 ppm), shrimp experience stress, leading to reduced feed intake, slower growth, and increased vulnerability to disease. In extreme cases, prolonged exposure to low DO levels can lead to shrimp suffocation and death.

2. **Impact on Exoskeleton Health:** Water chemistry, particularly pH, calcium, and salinity levels, plays a significant role in the health of the shrimp's exoskeleton. Shrimp undergo molting, a process in which they shed their old exoskeleton to grow a new, larger one. For healthy molting, shrimp require an environment with appropriate levels of calcium and magnesium, which contribute to the development of a strong, healthy

exoskeleton. pH levels in the water affect the availability of these minerals. An optimal pH range of 7.5 to 8.5 is recommended for shrimp farming to maintain proper mineral balance. If water pH is too low or too high, molting may be disrupted, leading to shell deformities and increased mortality.

6.1.2 Environmental Stressors and Shrimp Health

1. **Temperature Fluctuations:** Temperature is one of the most important environmental parameters affecting shrimp metabolism and immune function. The optimal temperature range for most shrimp species is between 25°C and 30°C (77°F to 86°F). When temperatures deviate from this range, shrimp experience stress, which impairs their growth and weakens their immune systems. At temperatures below 25°C, shrimp metabolism slows down, reducing feed conversion efficiency and growth rates. Conversely, higher

temperatures above 30°C can overstimulate metabolism, causing oxygen depletion and promoting the growth of harmful bacteria. Prolonged exposure to temperatures outside the ideal range makes shrimp more vulnerable to diseases and can result in mass mortality events.

2. **Toxins and Pollutants:** In shrimp farming, managing toxins such as ammonia, nitrites, and nitrates is essential to maintaining a healthy environment. These compounds are byproducts of shrimp waste, uneaten feed, and decomposing organic matter. Ammonia, in particular, is highly toxic to shrimp, especially in its un-ionized form (NH_3). Even at low concentrations, ammonia can cause gill damage, reducing shrimp's ability to absorb oxygen from the water. Nitrites (NO_2) interfere with hemolymph (shrimp blood) oxygen transport, leading to respiratory distress. Nitrates

(NO_3), though less toxic, can build up over time and contribute to poor water quality. Regular water changes, biological filtration, and proper feed management are necessary to prevent the accumulation of these toxic substances. Farmers should use water testing kits to regularly measure ammonia, nitrite, and nitrate levels and take corrective actions as needed.

6.1.3 Economic Impacts of Poor Water Quality

1. **Production Losses:** Poor water quality has a direct economic impact on shrimp farms. When water conditions deteriorate, shrimp experience stress, which compromises their growth, leading to stunted development and lower feed conversion efficiency. As a result, shrimp may take longer to reach market size, delaying harvest and increasing production costs. In severe cases, water quality issues can lead to mass die-offs, causing significant financial losses. Maintaining optimal water

conditions can help farmers achieve higher survival rates, faster growth, and better yields, improving farm profitability.

2. **Disease Outbreaks:** Deteriorating water quality creates an environment that encourages the proliferation of disease-causing organisms, including bacteria, viruses, and parasites. High levels of organic matter, toxins, and temperature fluctuations can weaken shrimp's immune systems, making them more susceptible to infections. Common diseases, such as White Spot Syndrome Virus (WSSV) and Vibrio infections, often thrive in poor water conditions. Disease outbreaks can spread rapidly across shrimp populations, leading to high mortality rates and the need for costly interventions such as antibiotics or water treatments. In some cases,

entire farming cycles may be lost due to disease outbreaks triggered by poor water management.

To avoid these problems, shrimp farmers must prioritize water quality management through regular monitoring and proactive interventions.

6.2 Monitoring and Managing Key Water Parameters

Effective water quality management is essential for the success of shrimp farming. Continuous monitoring and proper adjustment of water parameters ensure that shrimp have the optimal environment for growth, health, and disease resistance. Below are the most critical water quality parameters to monitor and manage:

6.2.1 Dissolved Oxygen (DO)

1. **Ideal DO Levels:** Shrimp require a sufficient supply of dissolved oxygen (DO) in the water to survive, thrive, and grow. Optimal DO levels for

shrimp farming range between 5-8 mg/L. When DO levels drop below this range, shrimp experience stress, leading to reduced feeding, slower growth, and increased vulnerability to disease. In extreme cases, low DO levels can cause shrimp mortality. Oxygen depletion is more likely to occur in densely stocked ponds or tanks, especially during hot weather or at night when oxygen production by aquatic plants decreases.

2. **Monitoring Tools:** To monitor DO levels, shrimp farmers can use devices such as DO meters and oxygen probes, which allow for real-time tracking of oxygen levels. Automated systems that continuously monitor DO levels can provide alerts when oxygen levels fall below the safe range, enabling quick interventions to prevent losses.

3. **Improving DO:** In cases of low dissolved oxygen, farmers can implement aeration systems to

maintain adequate DO levels. Common aeration solutions include:

- ✓ **Paddlewheels:** These aerators create surface movement that enhances oxygen transfer from the air to the water.
- ✓ **Diffused Air Systems:** Air diffusers release fine bubbles of oxygen into the water, increasing DO levels throughout the pond.
- ✓ **Emergency Aerators:** For sudden oxygen drops, emergency aerators provide quick oxygenation and prevent shrimp die-offs.

6.2.2 pH Levels

1. **Optimal pH Range:** Shrimp thrive in a slightly alkaline environment, with an ideal pH range of 7.5 to 8.5. A pH outside this range can negatively impact shrimp health and growth. Acidic conditions (pH below 7.5) can cause stress, interfere with shrimp metabolism, and impair molting, while overly alkaline water (pH above

8.5) can reduce the availability of essential minerals like calcium and magnesium, leading to exoskeleton problems.

2. **pH Monitoring:** Regular monitoring of pH is crucial to maintaining water balance. pH meters or test kits can be used to measure pH levels, with frequent testing recommended during feedings, water exchanges, and significant weather changes. Monitoring should be done daily or as conditions dictate.

3. **Correcting pH Imbalances:**
   - ✓ **To increase pH:** Adding lime (calcium carbonate or calcium hydroxide) can help raise pH levels in ponds or tanks.
   - ✓ **To decrease pH:** If water becomes too alkaline, organic acids such as citric acid or vinegar can be used to safely lower the pH to a desirable range.

6.2.3 Salinity

1. **Salinity Tolerance for Different Shrimp Species:** Salinity is another crucial factor for shrimp health. The ideal salinity range varies depending on the shrimp species:

   ✓ **Pacific white shrimp (Litopenaeus vannamei):** These shrimp thrive in salinity ranges between 10-35 ppt (parts per thousand).

   ✓ **Other species:** The optimal salinity range may differ for species like tiger shrimp or freshwater shrimp.

2. **Managing Salinity:** Salinity levels can fluctuate due to rainfall, evaporation, or water exchanges. Farmers can adjust salinity by:

   ✓ Diluting with freshwater to lower salinity in high-salinity environments.

   ✓ Adding salts (marine or synthetic) to increase salinity when levels fall too low. Farmers should frequently monitor salinity with refractometers or hydrometers and adjust as needed based on the species and location of the farm.

6.2.4 Temperature

1. Optimal Temperature Range: Temperature directly influences shrimp metabolism, immune function, and growth rates. Most shrimp species grow best in water temperatures between 25°C and 30°C (77°F to 86°F). Temperature fluctuations outside this range can cause stress, slow growth, impair immunity, and increase susceptibility to disease.

2. Temperature Monitoring and Control: Shrimp farmers should use thermometers, temperature sensors, or automated monitoring systems to track water temperatures regularly. For indoor farming systems, heaters and cooling systems can be installed to maintain consistent water temperatures. In outdoor farms, shading or water cooling measures may be needed during hot weather, while pond depth and circulation can help mitigate temperature fluctuations.

6.2.5 Ammonia, Nitrites, and Nitrates
1. Toxicity Thresholds:

- **Ammonia (NH3):** Ammonia is one of the most toxic substances in shrimp ponds. Concentrations above 0.05 mg/L are dangerous and can cause shrimp stress, reduced growth, and gill damage, eventually leading to death.
- **Nitrites (NO2):** Nitrites interfere with the ability of shrimp to transport oxygen in their hemolymph, leading to respiratory stress.
- **Nitrates (NO3):** Though less toxic, elevated nitrate levels can stress shrimp and negatively affect water quality.

2. Causes of Ammonia Build-Up: Ammonia levels increase due to shrimp waste, uneaten feed, and decaying organic matter. Poor pond management, overfeeding, and inadequate waste removal can exacerbate ammonia accumulation.

3. Managing Nitrogen Compounds: To control ammonia, nitrites, and nitrates, farmers can implement several strategies:

- ✓ **Biological filtration systems:** Biofilters containing nitrifying bacteria can convert toxic ammonia into less harmful nitrates.
- ✓ **Water changes:** Regular water changes help dilute toxic compounds, reducing the risk of ammonia and nitrite spikes.
- ✓ **Nitrifying bacteria supplements:** Adding commercial nitrifying bacteria can help accelerate the conversion of ammonia into nitrates.

6.2.6 Turbidity

1. Importance of Clear Water: Turbidity refers to water cloudiness caused by suspended particles such as algae, silt, and organic debris. High turbidity levels can reduce light penetration, affecting shrimp behavior and disrupting feeding patterns. Excess turbidity may also indicate poor water quality, as it is often associated with organic matter decomposition and oxygen depletion.

2. Managing Turbidity: To reduce turbidity and improve water clarity, farmers can:

- ✓ **Install sedimentation tanks:** These tanks allow suspended solids to settle before water enters the shrimp pond.
- ✓ **Use filters:** Mechanical filtration systems can remove suspended particles from the water.
- ✓ **Improve circulation:** Proper water circulation, through aerators or pumps, helps

prevent the buildup of turbidity-causing particles.

6.2.7 Alkalinity and Hardness

1. Effects on Shrimp Growth: Alkalinity (a measure of the water's ability to neutralize acids) and hardness (the concentration of calcium and magnesium) are essential for maintaining a stable environment for shrimp. Proper alkalinity levels (80-120 mg/L) help buffer pH changes, while adequate hardness ensures healthy molting and exoskeleton formation.

2. Monitoring and Adjusting Levels: Alkalinity and hardness should be monitored regularly, especially after water exchanges. If levels are too low, farmers can:

- ✓ Add lime or calcium carbonate to increase alkalinity and hardness. This ensures that shrimp have the necessary minerals for growth and molting, preventing stress and potential mortality.

6.3 Waste Management and Filtration Systems

Effective waste management plays a vital role in shrimp farming by ensuring that water quality remains optimal, preventing the accumulation of harmful substances, and supporting the long-term sustainability of the operation. Poor waste management can lead to the buildup of toxic compounds that can harm shrimp health, stunt growth, and cause disease outbreaks, which in turn affects farm productivity and profitability.

6.3.1 The Role of Waste Management in Shrimp Farming

In shrimp farming, organic waste comes from various sources, including uneaten feed, shrimp excretions, decaying organic matter, and dead shrimp. Left unmanaged, this organic load can lead to the rapid accumulation of harmful compounds such as ammonia, nitrites, and gases like hydrogen sulfide. These substances not only compromise water quality but also pose serious risks to shrimp health. Elevated levels of ammonia, for example, are highly toxic and can cause respiratory distress, while hydrogen sulfide can be lethal in high concentrations. Therefore, managing this waste is essential to maintaining a healthy environment for shrimp growth.

6.3.2 Mechanical Filtration Systems
Mechanical filtration systems play an important role in waste management by physically removing solid waste and debris from shrimp ponds or tanks. Screen filters are commonly used for this purpose, capturing larger particles and reducing the overall organic load in the water. Another option is sand filters, especially in recirculating aquaculture systems (RAS), where they help trap fine particles and improve water clarity and quality. However, for these systems to function effectively, regular maintenance is crucial. Clogged or

poorly maintained filters can become ineffective and even contribute to poor water quality, so routine cleaning and monitoring of filtration equipment are essential.

6.3.3 Biological Filtration Systems

Biological filtration systems are equally important, especially for managing nitrogen compounds like ammonia and nitrites, which are toxic to shrimp. Biofilters work by promoting the growth of beneficial bacteria that convert harmful ammonia into less toxic nitrates through the process of nitrification. This is a crucial step in preventing the buildup of toxic nitrogenous compounds in shrimp farming systems. Establishing a healthy population of nitrifying bacteria is key to maintaining effective biofiltration, and this can be facilitated by providing suitable substrates like gravel or specialized filter media, which offer a surface for bacterial colonization. Another approach to waste management in shrimp farming is Integrated Multi-Trophic Aquaculture (IMTA), where waste from shrimp is utilized by other organisms, such as algae or bivalves. This system not only helps manage waste but also creates a more self-sustaining ecosystem within the farm.

6.3.4 Water Recirculation and Exchange Systems
Water recirculation and exchange systems further aid in maintaining water quality. Recirculating Aquaculture Systems (RAS) are particularly advantageous as they reduce the need for constant water exchange by filtering and recycling water within the system. This minimizes water consumption, lowers the risk of introducing external contaminants, and helps maintain stable water quality parameters. Partial water exchange is another technique used in shrimp farming, where a portion of the water in the pond or tank is replaced periodically to remove excess waste and refresh the water environment.

6.3.5 Sedimentation and Settling Ponds

Sedimentation and settling ponds are designed to handle solid waste that escapes filtration systems. These ponds are specifically designed to allow suspended solids to settle out of the water before it re-enters the shrimp ponds or tanks. Regular dredging of sedimentation ponds is necessary to remove accumulated waste and prevent it from recontaminating the farm's water system. Wastewater treatment is an essential aspect of modern shrimp farming, particularly in farms where water reuse is a priority. Wastewater treatment systems use aeration, biofilters, and sometimes chemical treatments to remove toxins and harmful substances from farm effluent before it is discharged or recycled. Recycling treated water back into the farm can significantly reduce water consumption, lower costs, and minimize the environmental impact of shrimp farming.

CHAPTER 7

HARVESTING AND POST-HARVEST CARE

7.1 Timing the Harvest: Signs of Shrimp Readiness

Harvest timing plays a critical role in ensuring optimal shrimp yield, product quality, and profitability. If harvested too early, the shrimp may be undersized, reducing their market value. On the other hand, delaying the harvest can lead to overcrowding, poor water quality, or disease outbreaks, all of which could affect the final product. Therefore, understanding the right time to harvest involves careful monitoring of shrimp growth, behavior, physical characteristics, and environmental conditions.

7.1.1 Growth Monitoring

To accurately time the harvest, regular monitoring of shrimp growth is essential. This ensures that shrimp have reached the desired market size and weight, and allows for optimal financial returns.

- **Growth Rate and Size Targets:** The growth rate of shrimp depends on several factors, including the species being farmed, environmental conditions such as water temperature and quality, and the feeding regime. Typically, shrimp are harvested when they reach a size of 20-25 grams, but the exact size target can vary based on market demands. Some markets may prefer smaller shrimp, while others favor larger specimens. By regularly tracking growth rates, farmers can predict when the shrimp will reach the desired size and plan their harvest accordingly.

- **Sampling and Size Assessment:** To monitor shrimp growth accurately, it's important to periodically sample shrimp from different locations within the pond or tank. Sampling gives insight into the overall health and consistency of the shrimp population. By taking size measurements from multiple areas, farmers can ensure that the majority of shrimp have reached the optimal market size. This helps avoid harvesting when there is significant size variation among the shrimp, which can reduce product uniformity and marketability.

7.1.2 Behavioral and Physical Indicators

Shrimp exhibit specific behavioral and physical signs when they approach harvest readiness. Recognizing these signs allows for a more precise harvest schedule.

- **Behavioral Signs of Maturity:** As shrimp mature, their feeding behavior tends to slow down.

This is because they are nearing the end of their growth cycle and require less food. Decreased feed consumption is often a good indicator that shrimp are nearing harvest size. Additionally, mature shrimp tend to move less actively, another sign that they are reaching full development. Monitoring feeding patterns and activity levels can therefore provide valuable clues about when the shrimp are ready for harvest.

- **Physical Changes:** Shrimp that are ready for harvest will also show noticeable physical changes. A fully developed shrimp will have a firm body texture, which indicates that its muscles and exoskeleton have fully matured. The coloration of the exoskeleton becomes clear and strong, often reflecting the species' typical colors more vividly. These physical characteristics signal that the shrimp have reached their peak development, and harvesting them at this stage will result in a high-quality product.

7.1.3 Environmental Considerations

Environmental factors such as temperature, water quality, and seasonal changes can influence the optimal timing of the shrimp harvest. Understanding these factors helps farmers schedule the harvest to minimize risks and maximize yields.

- **Seasonal Timing:** In many regions, shrimp farming is influenced by seasonal variations in temperature, water quality, and other environmental conditions. For example, in tropical regions, shrimp tend to grow faster during the warmer months, while in cooler climates, growth may slow down as water temperatures drop. By aligning the harvest with the shrimp's natural growth cycle and considering seasonal changes, farmers can optimize the timing to ensure the highest possible yields. Seasonal factors also affect the market, as shrimp prices can fluctuate based on supply and demand at different times of the year.

- **Water Quality Before Harvest:** Maintaining stable water quality is essential in the days leading up to the harvest. Factors such as pH, salinity, dissolved oxygen, and ammonia levels must be carefully monitored to ensure that the shrimp remain healthy and stress-free. Harvesting in poor water conditions can result in stressed or weakened shrimp, which not only reduces their quality but also increases the risk of mortality during the harvesting process. Ensuring stable water quality minimizes stress on the shrimp and helps preserve their health, size, and overall product quality.

7.2 Harvesting Techniques for Maximum Yield

Selecting the appropriate harvesting technique is essential for shrimp farmers aiming to maximize yield, minimize shrimp stress, and ensure that shrimp quality is preserved during collection. The chosen method will depend on factors like farm size, infrastructure, shrimp species, and market demands. By employing the right technique, farmers can ensure an efficient and smooth harvesting process.

7.2.1 Partial vs. Full Harvesting

Different harvesting strategies can be employed based on production cycles and market conditions. Deciding between partial or full harvesting largely depends on the farm's operational goals and the growth stage of the shrimp.

- **Partial Harvesting:** This method involves harvesting a portion of the shrimp population while allowing the remaining shrimp to continue growing. Partial harvesting is particularly useful in staggered production systems, where a farmer may wish to supply different shrimp sizes to meet varied market demands. By leaving some shrimp in the pond or tank to grow longer, farmers can optimize their production cycles and increase yields over time. Additionally, partial harvesting can help avoid overcrowding, ensuring that the shrimp left behind have ample space and resources to continue thriving.

- **Full Harvesting:** Full harvesting is typically employed in larger farms or when the entire pond or tank is due for turnover. This method ensures that all shrimp are harvested at once, making it easier to coordinate post-harvest processing and transportation. Full harvesting is often necessary when the shrimp have all reached market size, or when water conditions require the complete emptying of the pond. This method requires efficient planning and logistical coordination to prevent delays that could impact shrimp quality, particularly during transport and processing.

7.2.2 Drain Harvesting

Drain harvesting is a widely used technique, especially in outdoor pond systems, allowing farmers to gather shrimp by manipulating water levels.

- **Traditional Pond Harvesting:** In outdoor ponds, shrimp are often harvested by slowly draining the pond over a set period. As the water level decreases, shrimp naturally move toward a central catch basin or sump area, where they can be easily collected using nets or mechanical pumps. This method allows for the efficient collection of a large number of shrimp without the need for extensive labor.

- **Advantages and Considerations:** One of the primary advantages of drain harvesting is its simplicity and effectiveness for large shrimp populations. It is particularly suitable for full harvests. However, controlling the drainage speed and water level is critical. Draining the pond too quickly can stress or injure the shrimp, reducing their quality. Properly managing the drainage process helps ensure that shrimp remain calm, minimizing stress, injury, and mortality.

7.2.3 Cast Netting and Seine Netting

For smaller or mid-sized farms, manual methods such as cast netting and seine netting can be employed to collect shrimp. These methods are more labor-intensive but can offer a high degree of control over the harvesting process.

- **Cast Net Harvesting:** Cast nets are circular nets with weighted edges that are manually thrown into the water. This method is particularly suited to small-scale shrimp farms or tank systems where shrimp are kept in confined spaces. Though labor-intensive, cast netting allows for precise collection, reducing the risk of shrimp injury. It is also beneficial when only a small portion of the shrimp population needs to be harvested, making it ideal for partial harvesting on a smaller scale.

- **Seine Net Harvesting:** A seine net is a large net that is dragged across the pond or tank to capture shrimp. Seine nets are often used in mid-sized farms, where larger quantities of shrimp need to be collected. This technique requires careful handling to avoid damaging the shrimp. By maintaining proper tension and control over the net, farmers can minimize injury and maximize yield. Seine netting is effective for gathering shrimp over a wide area and is especially useful for partial harvests in larger ponds.

7.2.4 Pump Harvesting

Modern, mechanized farms often use pump systems for shrimp collection, particularly in indoor or tank-based aquaculture systems.

- **Mechanical Harvesting:** In high-tech shrimp farms, mechanical pumps can be used to siphon shrimp from tanks or ponds into holding containers. This method is especially useful in Recirculating Aquaculture Systems (RAS) or other controlled environments where traditional methods like nets are impractical. Mechanical pumps are designed to minimize damage to shrimp during the transfer process. These pumps are often equipped with gentle suction and smooth tubing to reduce the risk of harming the shrimp's delicate exoskeleton.

- **Benefits of Pump Systems:** Pump harvesting allows for rapid and efficient shrimp collection, reducing the time required to complete the harvest. This method is particularly beneficial for large-scale operations where quick collection is needed to maintain shrimp quality. However, pump systems require a significant investment in specialized equipment. Additionally, careful management is needed during the transfer process to ensure that shrimp are not exposed to prolonged stress, as this could affect their quality and market value.

7.2.5 Key Considerations for Harvesting

To ensure a successful harvest, it's important to take several factors into account, regardless of the method used:

- **Minimizing Shrimp Stress:** Shrimp are highly sensitive to stress, which can affect their health and quality. Gentle handling and proper timing of the harvest help reduce stress levels and maintain shrimp integrity.

- **Post-Harvest Handling:** After harvesting, shrimp should be quickly processed or stored in cool conditions to preserve freshness and prevent deterioration. Delays in post-harvest handling can lead to poor product quality.

- **Infrastructure:** The choice of harvesting method often depends on the farm's infrastructure. For example, large-scale farms with sophisticated water management systems may prefer drain or pump harvesting, while smaller farms may opt for manual methods like cast or seine netting.

- **Labor and Costs:** Manual methods require more labor but may be less expensive in terms of equipment. However, mechanized systems like pump harvesting reduce labor costs and time but involve higher initial investments.

7.3 Post-Harvest Handling and Quality Control

Effective post-harvest handling and quality control are crucial steps in ensuring that shrimp remain fresh, healthy, and marketable after they have been harvested. Proper care in these processes not only preserves the quality of the product but also maximizes its shelf life and market value. Poor handling can lead to physical damage, increased stress, or spoilage, resulting in financial losses. Here is a detailed exploration of essential post-harvest practices and quality control measures:

7.3.1 De-stressing and Resting

Shrimp experience considerable stress during harvesting, which can negatively affect their meat quality and survival. Managing this stress immediately after harvest is essential to maintaining the overall health and marketability of the shrimp.

- **Post-Harvest Stress Management:** Shrimp can become agitated and stressed during the harvest process, particularly if handled roughly or if they experience sudden changes in their environment, such as a drop in water levels or temperature. Stress can lead to higher mortality rates and reduced meat quality due to increased metabolic activity and energy consumption. To mitigate this, harvested shrimp should be placed in holding tanks filled with clean, well-aerated water for several hours after the harvest. This resting period helps them recover from the stress of harvesting, stabilizing their health before they undergo further processing.
- **Temperature Management:** Temperature plays a vital role in maintaining shrimp quality after harvest. Shrimp should be kept at controlled, cool temperatures to slow their metabolic

processes and reduce stress. If shrimp are not immediately processed after harvest, maintaining them at lower temperatures is crucial to prevent spoilage and maintain freshness. During transport and storage, temperatures must be monitored to avoid fluctuations that could harm the shrimp.

7.3.2 Sorting and Grading

Once shrimp have been harvested and allowed to rest, they need to be sorted and graded to meet specific market standards. Size and quality grading are important steps that help ensure uniformity and maximize market value.

- **Size Grading:** After harvest, shrimp are typically graded by size to meet the preferences of different markets. Larger shrimp often fetch higher prices, so sorting them by size categories allows farmers to maximize their profits. This can be done either manually or using specialized grading machines.

Consistent size grading also makes it easier for retailers to present the shrimp in a standardized way to consumers, contributing to better marketability.

- **Quality Assessment:** During the grading process, shrimp should be inspected for any signs of physical damage, disease, or deformities. Physical damage may include cracked or broken exoskeletons, which can affect the shrimp's appearance and reduce their value. Any shrimp showing signs of disease or poor health should be removed from the batch. These shrimp may be sold at a lower price or used for alternative purposes, such as being processed into shrimp meal. The goal is to ensure that only healthy, undamaged shrimp reach the consumer market, as this guarantees a premium product and minimizes losses.

7.3.3 Handling and Cleaning

Proper handling and cleaning are critical in preserving shrimp quality after harvest. Rough or careless handling can lead to physical damage, while inadequate cleaning can result in bacterial growth, reducing the shrimp's shelf life and posing potential health risks to consumers.

- **Gentle Handling:** To minimize physical damage to the shrimp, it is essential to use soft, non-abrasive tools and containers during the post-harvest handling process. Shrimp have a delicate exoskeleton, which can crack or break easily if handled too roughly. The use of padded containers, soft nets, and careful movement of shrimp from one stage to the next helps maintain their quality and appearance. Physical damage not only reduces the shrimp's market value but also increases their susceptibility to infection.

- **Cleaning:** Once shrimp are harvested, they need to be thoroughly cleaned to remove debris, excess feed, or bacteria that may be present on their bodies. This step is crucial in maintaining the quality of the shrimp during transport and storage. Cleaning typically involves rinsing the shrimp with clean, cold water immediately after harvest. Cold water helps slow bacterial growth while also removing dirt, sediment, and other contaminants. Proper cleaning ensures that the shrimp are safe for consumption and maintain their freshness for longer periods.

7.3.4 Importance of Cold Chain Management

An integral part of post-harvest handling is maintaining an unbroken cold chain from the moment of harvest to the point of sale. This involves keeping the shrimp at the correct low temperature throughout all stages of transport and storage to preserve their freshness and prevent spoilage.

- **Rapid Cooling:** After sorting and grading, shrimp must be cooled quickly to prevent bacterial growth. Ideally, shrimp should be placed on ice or stored in chilled seawater at temperatures between 0°C and 4°C. The quicker shrimp are cooled, the longer they will stay fresh. Some farms and processing plants use ice slurry systems to rapidly cool the shrimp while simultaneously washing away any surface contaminants.

- **Storage and Transport:** Maintaining the cold chain throughout the entire logistics process is critical. Shrimp should be stored in insulated containers with adequate amounts of ice or in refrigerated trucks to ensure consistent temperatures during transportation to processing plants or markets. Temperature fluctuations during transport can lead to a reduction in shrimp quality, so careful monitoring is essential.

7.3.5 Quality Control and Shelf-Life Preservation

Quality control measures must be in place to ensure that harvested shrimp meet the highest standards for freshness, taste, and appearance. These steps are crucial for maximizing the shelf life of shrimp and ensuring consumer satisfaction.

- **Sensory Evaluation:** Regular sensory evaluation helps assess the shrimp's freshness and quality. This includes checking for firmness of the flesh, color consistency, and odor. Fresh shrimp should have a mild, ocean-like smell, firm texture, and bright coloration. Any signs of spoilage, such as a strong fishy odor or soft texture, indicate that the shrimp are no longer fit for sale.

- **Packaging for Freshness:** Packaging is another critical factor in preserving shrimp quality. Shrimp should be packaged in a way that minimizes their exposure to air and light, both of which can contribute to spoilage. Vacuum-sealing or using modified atmosphere packaging (MAP) are common techniques used to extend the shelf life of shrimp by reducing the growth of bacteria and maintaining freshness.

- **Traceability Systems:** Traceability systems are becoming increasingly important in the seafood industry to ensure that shrimp are handled according to sustainability and food safety standards. By employing tracking technologies such as barcoding or blockchain, shrimp farmers can provide detailed records of the shrimp's journey from farm to market, ensuring that quality control measures are followed at every step.

7.4 Packaging and Transport for Market

Proper packaging and transportation of shrimp are crucial steps in maintaining their freshness, quality, and overall marketability. The goal is to ensure that the shrimp reach their destination in the best possible condition, whether they are being sold fresh or frozen. Key elements include effective chilling or freezing, suitable packaging methods, efficient transport logistics, and appealing market presentation. Here's a detailed expansion of these critical processes:

7.4.1 Chilling and Freezing
1. Chilling Fresh Shrimp

- **Chilling in Ice:** Freshly harvested shrimp are highly perishable and begin to degrade rapidly if not cooled immediately. To preserve their freshness, they are typically placed in ice right after harvest. This rapid chilling lowers their body temperature, slowing down metabolic processes and preventing the growth of bacteria and other microorganisms that can cause spoilage. The shrimp should be kept at temperatures close to 0°C (32°F), as this ensures they remain fresh during short-term storage or transport.

- **Ice-to-Shrimp Ratio:** For effective chilling, it is important to maintain the right ratio of ice to shrimp. A common practice is to use about a 1:1 ice-to-shrimp ratio, but this may vary depending on the ambient temperature and transport conditions. The ice should also be food-grade and replaced as needed to maintain consistent cold temperatures.

2. Freezing for Long-Term Storage

- **Flash-Freezing:** Shrimp intended for long-distance transport or long-term storage are usually frozen to maintain their quality over extended periods. Freezing can preserve the shrimp's freshness for months, but the method used matters significantly. Flash-freezing techniques like Individually Quick Frozen (IQF) are often preferred. IQF shrimp are rapidly frozen individually, which helps retain their natural texture, color, and flavor. This method also prevents the shrimp from clumping together, making it easier to handle and portion out later.

- **Freezing Temperatures:** For effective freezing, shrimp should be frozen at temperatures of -18°C (0°F) or lower. Maintaining this low temperature during both storage and transport ensures that the shrimp retain their quality without any degradation. The longer the shrimp are stored, the more critical it becomes to maintain consistent freezing conditions.

7.4.2 Packaging Methods
1. Vacuum Sealing

- **Benefits of Vacuum Sealing:** Vacuum-sealing is one of the most effective packaging methods for both fresh and frozen shrimp. By removing the air from the packaging, vacuum-sealing reduces the oxidation that can lead to spoilage, discoloration, and a loss of flavor. The lack of oxygen also inhibits the growth of bacteria, extending the shrimp's shelf life. Vacuum-sealing is particularly common for frozen shrimp, as it ensures that they remain fresh even during extended storage.
- **Materials and Methods:** The packaging material used for vacuum-sealing should be high-quality, food-grade plastic that is resistant to tearing and puncturing. Automated vacuum-sealing machines are typically employed, ensuring an airtight seal that preserves the shrimp's quality.

2. Ice Packing

- **Ice Layers in Insulated Containers:** For shrimp that are sold fresh, packing with layers of ice is a traditional method. Fresh shrimp are placed in insulated containers, and ice is layered between them to keep the temperature low during transport. The containers used should be insulated to prevent the ice from melting too quickly. This method works well for short-term storage and transport over shorter distances.
- **Avoiding Cross-Contamination:** One key consideration in ice packing is preventing cross-contamination between the shrimp and the ice. This can be achieved by ensuring the ice is food-grade and checking for any leaks in the packaging that could allow the shrimp to come into contact with meltwater or contaminants.

7.4.3 Transport Logistics
1. Cold Chain Management

- **Maintaining Consistent Cold Chain:** The cold chain refers to the series of temperature-controlled steps from harvest to market. Whether shrimp are fresh or frozen, maintaining a consistent cold chain is essential for preserving quality. For fresh shrimp, the temperature should remain close to 0°C (32°F), while frozen shrimp should be kept at -18°C (0°F) or lower. Any break in the cold chain can cause temperature fluctuations that lead to bacterial growth, spoilage, or a loss in product quality.
- **Refrigerated Trucks and Containers:** During transport, refrigerated trucks or containers with built-in temperature controls are used to maintain the cold chain. These vehicles are equipped with cooling systems that ensure the shrimp stay at the correct temperature from the moment they leave the farm until they reach the market or processing

plant. Proper monitoring systems, such as thermometers and alarms, help ensure that any temperature deviations are detected and corrected quickly.

7.4.4 Minimizing Transport Time

- **Efficiency in Logistics:** The less time shrimp spend in transit, the better their condition upon arrival. Prolonged transport times can increase the risk of spoilage or quality degradation, particularly for fresh shrimp. Therefore, logistical planning should prioritize speed and efficiency, ensuring that shrimp are transported to their destination as quickly as possible. Minimizing delays and optimizing routes for delivery can help ensure that shrimp reach markets or processing plants while still in peak condition.

- **Transport Safety:** Care should also be taken to prevent physical damage during transport. Rough handling or vibrations during transportation can lead to bruising or breaking of the shrimp's exoskeleton, reducing their market value.

7.4.5 Market Preparation and Presentation
1. Labeling and Certification

- **Accurate and Clear Labeling:** Proper labeling of shrimp is critical for both regulatory compliance and consumer information. Each package should be labeled with key details such as the farm of origin, harvest date, and size category. In some markets, additional certifications may be required or desirable, such as organic, sustainable farming, or fair-trade labels. These certifications can provide shrimp with a competitive advantage in certain markets, particularly among consumers who prioritize environmentally friendly and ethical sourcing.

- **Traceability and Compliance:** Ensuring traceability in the packaging process helps maintain food safety standards. This is important for tracking the shrimp through the supply chain in case of a recall or food safety concern. Many modern packaging systems include barcodes or QR codes that provide consumers and regulators with detailed information about the product's origin and handling.

2. Attractive Presentation

- **Consistent Sizing and Neat Packing:** In competitive markets, the visual appeal of the shrimp can have a significant impact on sales. Buyers prefer shrimp that are consistent in size, neatly packed, and have a clean appearance. To enhance marketability, shrimp should be sorted and packed so that they look uniform. This consistency is particularly important for retail packaging, where consumers often base their purchasing decisions on the product's visual appeal.

- **Packaging Design:** The packaging itself should also be designed to catch the buyer's attention while offering protection. Transparent sections in packaging allow buyers to inspect the shrimp before purchasing, while the design and labeling can highlight features like sustainability certifications or premium quality.

CONCLUSION

Shrimp farming, like any agricultural endeavor, requires dedication, careful planning, and a deep understanding of the environment and species being cultivated. As we've explored throughout this book, mastering the various aspects of shrimp farming—from setting up your farm and managing water quality to providing optimal nutrition and ensuring shrimp health—is essential for achieving success. By following the guidelines and strategies outlined in this book, whether you're a beginner starting out with a small operation or an experienced farmer looking to scale up, you are equipped with the knowledge and tools to build a sustainable and profitable shrimp farm. The focus on maintaining water quality, implementing biosecurity measures, and adopting sustainable practices not only ensures the well-being of your shrimp but also contributes to the long-term health of the environment

As the global demand for shrimp continues to grow, shrimp farming offers a promising opportunity for farmers willing to invest in quality management and sustainable practices. This industry is evolving rapidly, and staying updated with the latest research and technological advancements will be key to remaining competitive. Your shrimp farming journey will inevitably face challenges, but with perseverance, continuous learning, and a commitment to excellence, you can create a thriving business that supports both economic growth and environmental stewardship. Remember, success in shrimp farming comes not just from understanding the biology of shrimp but from applying that knowledge with care, precision, and a focus on sustainability.

May this guide serve as a valuable resource and reference throughout your shrimp farming endeavors, helping you navigate the complexities of the industry and achieve lasting success.

Made in the USA
Coppell, TX
26 February 2025